SUCCESS BASICS

WEALTH AND GENEROSITY

Beth Jones

19 18 17 16   10 9 8 7 6 5 4 3 2 1

Success Basics: Wealth and Generosity
ISBN 13: 978-168031-059-7
Copyright © 2016 by Beth Jones
www.bethjones.org

Published by Harrison House Publishers
Tulsa, OK 74145
www.harrisonhouse.com

CONTENTS

INTRODUCTION

Okay, friends, are you ready for your financial life to take on a new trajectory?

I am so excited in my spirit about sharing this book with you because the things you are about to study have the potential to do just that—to launch your life and your future in a new direction. If you read, study, and meditate on the Scriptures we are about to explore, I know the Holy Spirit will answer basic questions you have had about wealth and generosity, as well as put things into a fresh and eternal perspective and inspire your faith!

Many of you who have been through my *Getting a Grip on the Basics* series over the years are like old friends. We've been down a few roads in God's Word, haven't we? Others of you are new to my books, so you are new friends whom I look forward to meeting, if not here on earth, then one day in heaven.

Whether old or new friends, you all are in my heart as I sit down to type and share principles about living in God's economy. You'll notice this book *(and all the books in the Success Basics series)* follows the workbook style teaching you've grown accustomed to, but it has been combined with more stories and fun! There will be an ebb and flow. One minute I'll be sharing real-life stories with you, and the next minute we'll jump into line-upon-line teaching looking up numerous scriptures, filling in blanks, and listening to what the Spirit wants us to know. I am passionate about helping you get the basics while enjoying the process, so I'll do my best to keep it personal, encouraging and motivating.

I hope you enjoy this series of books as you continue to *get a grip* on the basics!

I believe at the end of our study together, you'll have a strong foundation and many practical helps. You'll experience something that will forever change your life. Living a life where wealth and generosity go hand-in-hand won't be just the greatest sounding theory; it will be your reality.

In our four sessions, we will cover these basics:

- The Life of Wealth and Generosity
- The Blessing of the Tithe
- The Multiplied Fruit of Offerings
- The Investment of Alms

OUR GOALS FOR THIS BOOK

In this book, we have two goals as we study God's Word.

First, let's embrace God's will and desire to help us get wealth.

Second, let's respond to God's generosity towards us by using our wealth to be generous towards Him, His church and His people.

When we renew our minds to what God's Word says, we discover that it's the blessing of the Lord that makes a person rich, and it's not wrong, immoral, worldly, selfish, or covetous for a Christian to be wealthy. In fact, it's something you should desire! (What? I know for some of you, your brain just went tilt. But stay with me, and let's get into the Word.)

Remember, God loves you and wants you blessed and He wants you to be a blessing. It's a simple fact; we cannot give what we do not have. We may want to be generous, but if we are not wealthy at some level, we don't have the means to be generous. That's why it's so imperative that Christians become convinced from God's Word that He wants them to get wealth in order to enjoy life and to be generous. (Thank you, 1 Timothy 6:17.)

Clearly our beliefs, faith, and views need to be based on the truth of God's Word, not on our own experiences or opinions or the expertise of others. The best way to know God's will on any topic is to get into the Bible and study the Word like the Bereans did in Acts 17:11 (KJV), "These were more noble than those in Thessalonica, in that they received the word with all readiness of mind, and searched the scriptures daily, whether those things were so." In other words, the Bereans didn't just take at face value that what the apostle Paul or anyone else said was the truth; they studied the Scriptures themselves to be sure what they were hearing was true. As you go through each session, be sure to study your own Bible and look up the scriptures for yourself to be sure you are personally convinced of God's will on the subject of wealth and generosity.

To do this objectively, you may have to take off your traditional way of thinking and possibly unlearn some things you previously believed to be true. We can all fall into the trap of honoring traditions more than God's Word, so keep in mind what Jesus told His disciples when He said that the "traditions of men" make the Word of God of no effect (Matthew 15:6; Mark 7:13).

To get the most out of this book, let me encourage you with three quick instructions.

1. Pray

"Father, I ask You to open my eyes to all You want to do in me and through me. I pray for the spirit of wisdom and understanding as I learn more about wealth and generosity and what it means to live in Your economy. Thank You in advance for the revelation and insights I need. In Jesus Name. Amen."

2. Start Now

Don't put this book in the "I should do this someday" pile. Make a decision to get started now. All you need is an open heart, your Bible, and a pen. (Because there are lots of blanks to fill in!)

3. Expect

Fasten your seatbelt. Expect God to take you on a wonderful ride in His Word and into a greater experience of gaining wealth and being more generous than you thought possible.

Okay, friends, are you ready? Here we go.

START HERE: MY STORY

———————

Who am I to write a book on wealth and generosity? There are plenty of people wealthier and more generous than I, who could write such a book!

Perhaps the reason God put this topic on my heart is because I am probably a lot like many of you, a normal person who didn't start out wealthy or generous. Eventually, I came to understand how incredibly generous God has been and continues to be towards me, and I had a desire to respond to His kindness. When I began to learn about His desire to prosper my life, to help me succeed, and to increase my wealth, I was surprised! This was not the buzzkill God I had heard about. When I started to understand the joy of giving and the blessings and rewards attached to tithes, offerings, and alms—I (and when I got married, my husband and I) entered into the flow of God's economy. It gives me great joy to share these simple basics with you, dear friend!

I could have written this book strictly based on the Word from the theoretical angle, and it would be true, because God's Word is truth. But now, after 30 years of walking with the Lord and employing these principles, I can promise you based on the authority of God's Word and from my personal experience, He wants to help you get wealth so you enjoy life and are free to give generously. Not only will you enjoy what you are about to study, it will work in your life! I want to emphasize this—you will love it, and it will work! (I know. I sound dramatic.) I am slightly enthusiastic about this topic because I know what happened in my life as I got ahold of these wealth and generosity basics. I promise you the Lord wants the same for you! (Don't get tripped up on the word "wealth"—we'll give it a proper definition in Session 1.)

PROMISES, PROMISES!

Promises are a big deal. Aren't there thousands of books promising success, wealth, abundance, hundredfold harvest, the millionaire's secret, or easy steps to becoming a billionaire? The truth is, there's no "get rich quick scheme" that has any value. But God has given us dozens of instructions and promises regarding His desire for our wealth and generosity.

Tapping into God's plan for wealth and generosity is not a magic bullet; it's a lifestyle and this, my friend, may cause you to have a "love/hate" relationship with God's promises on this subject. Kinda like the love/hate experience my family had when I promised them they would love camping in the tent-cabins at Colter Bay near the Grand Tetons of Wyoming—when in fact, I had never been camping there, nor had our family ever camped once in our existence. Perhaps this little story will prepare you for the rest of the book.

I knew we were in trouble when my husband and I pulled our minivan, filled to the brim with four teenagers, up to our campsite and saw a small tent-cabin (yes, it's exactly that: a tent-cabin) and a small bonfire pit. (Keywords: Everything. Was. Small. We are a giant family of six—kin to Shrek—each hovering near six feet or more.) When our campsite neighbors pulled up and began to unload their multiple tubs of Rubbermaid camping gear complete with tents, screens, a propane stove, and lanterns, my children stared at me with dagger-like eyes. Fine. So, we didn't have a stove, flashlight, utensils, plates, food, or matches. We had a pocketknife. But this was nothing a trip to the camp store couldn't fix. Two packages of hot dogs later, along with stale buns and a few packets of ketchup and mustard we "stole" from the deli, and we were living like pioneers! Never mind we had to borrow matches from our professional camping neighbors to start our bonfire. The non-stop disapproving body language I felt from my loving family as we moved in should have discouraged me, but I knew eventually they would love this whole experience!

Well, our three-day camping experience turned into a one night *get us the heck out of here* experience. Other than the fact that we spent the night in a World War II era tent-cabin where the wood-burning heater ran out of wood around 2 a.m., the temperature dropped to 32 degrees, and we were all freezing, it wasn't a big deal. I hardly noticed the frostbite because of the shooting pain in my torn rotator cuff that zapped me every time I tried to roll over in my 1940s army cot. Besides, who could sleep? I was still thinking about the "watch out for the hungry bears late at night" comment I'd heard at the camp store earlier. Not to worry, I was pretty sure the shouts from our cabin sent every bear in three counties running for cover at 2:15 a.m. when my husband woke up to stoke the woodless fire and tripped over our boys who were sleeping soundly in soccer chairs. When they collapsed under dad's falling body, their freaked-out screams likely started a flurry of bears texting one another, "Crazy Alert: Stay away from Site 37."

Somehow the girls slept through the chaos, but in the morning, their parsed-lip mumbles about having to pay 25 cents to take a shower in a grimy stall didn't go unnoticed. Trying to be chipper, I reminded them, "C'mon you guys! This is how the Little House on the Prairie people did it!" Eyes were rolling. By the time we packed up our goods and pulled out of the campground, I'd had enough of the bad attitudes and forced the entire family to sing, "You've got to get up every morning with a smile on your face and show the world all the love in your heart." (Thank you Carole King, Tapestry Album, 1970s.)

Do you know, once we saw the Grand Tetons and hiked up beautiful trails to see mountain views and waterfalls, not to mention the moose, bears, and plentiful wildlife (from a distance!), the entire family was singing my praises about what a great vacation this was! So, here's the punch line. I promised they would love camping and to this day, the Colter Bay camping experience is the one and only vacation our family still raves, mocks, and reenacts all of these years later. (I knew they would love it!)

That is what I am telling you, dear friends. I promise you will love getting into God's Word to learn about wealth and generosity and the fruit that results. Even if at first it's a love/hate relationship, even if it's exciting and uncomfortable at the same time, even if you think you have no desire to obtain wealth or be generous, even if you hate talking about money, even if you don't want to give a dime to anyone or are afraid some crazy, greedy preacher will try to manipulate you, even when you put it into practice and then it seems like nothing happens (or it looks worse) and you have to exercise your faith and patience longer than you planned (and that is always the case), I promise you'll love this topic! Soon enough, you'll be raving and reenacting these things for many years to come!

MY REFERENCE POINTS
MIGHT BE A LOT LIKE YOURS

I think it's important for you to hear about my journey as it relates to wealth and generosity, because I believe it will give you hope and inspiration for your own life. Here's a little bit of my story.

I grew up on the clearance rack. Literally, that's how we were raised. My mother was the Queen of Clearance and was once asked if she had ever bought anything that was not on clearance. Her "Dear Lord, I hope not!" response perfectly described our childhood and mindset. It never occurred to me to even look at the full price racks, let alone buy anything from those racks. That was for other folk.

Being raised by a single mom meant money was tight, but my three sisters and I had enough money for the essentials: Cocoa Krispies and Capt'n Crunch. I did the grocery shopping for our family when I was in high school, and I remember seeing the rich people buying colorful Del Monte canned fruit. I just knew that one day we too would be able to afford Del Monte! I had learned the art of filling two shopping carts for under a hundred dollars. Of course, most of our products were not Del Monte but the black and white brand—I later discovered "generic" was the proper term. I was a bargain shopper. I knew how to be frugal and budget-conscious, and we always had the essentials. I never felt poor. I never felt rich. I thought we were in the middle.

I'll never forget the moment I crossed over in my thinking about money.

Up until that point, I was not a tither. I had not given any money to a church or ministry that I remember. I might have given small change to the poor, but maybe not. In other words, I didn't know a thing about God's wealth and generosity or God's economic laws, and I was not a giver.

If anything, I might have been considered a thief (unintentional, of course). It started in seventh grade when I stole Marlboro cigarettes from my mom. Eventually, I figured out how to fund my own cigarette habit by collecting enough pop and beer cans to turn in to stores for the ten-cent refunds they offered.

My most dastardly deed of thievery happened in high school, when I saw an ad in the *Tiger Beat* teen magazine and signed up for the Columbia Records "Get 12 Albums for $1.00" offer. I selected all of my favorite albums (albums are made of vinyl; you can find them in thrift stores), and I was thrilled to receive them in the mail to begin my record collection. The only problem was that part of this offer was my agreement to purchase six more albums over the next three years, at full price. Well, somehow I conveniently forgot that part and never fulfilled my end of the bargain. I just enjoyed my twelve albums for $1.00. (Years later when I became a Christian, the Lord dealt with me on this "robbery" and I sent Columbia Records an apology letter and offered to pay them for my crime. Graciously, they sent me a letter to state they appreciated my honesty and forgave my debt. That, my friends, is unmerited favor!)

After my freshman year of college at the ripe age of 19, my college roommate and childhood friend introduced me to Jesus, and I invited Him into my life and became a born-again Christian. I still didn't have any money and I didn't know very much about God other than "with God all things are possible," but as a new believer, I saw God perform two significant financial wonders for me. These all led up to my crossing-over moment.

I was all of six months old as a Christian, and the Lord prompted me to sign up for a spring break evangelism week at Daytona Beach with my new Campus Crusade for Christ friends. (Full disclosure, I may have actually prompted myself when I heard it was a trip to Daytona Beach!) The first thing our Campus Crusade leader told me was that I would have to raise my own funds of $100 for this trip, so he encouraged me to send a support letter to all the Christians I knew. As a brand new Christian, I knew exactly zero other Christians—well, except for the bank president I had just read about while writing a paper for a class at school about the "Born-Again Movement." I was reading *Time Magazine* and saw a story of a Christian man who was a bank president in Chattanooga (which I quoted in my paper), so I sent him a letter to see if he would want to sponsor my trip with Campus Crusade for Christ. He was the only person I "knew," and as a bank president, he certainly fell under the "I might be able to support you" category. Well, lo and behold, within one week he sent me a personal check for $100 to cover my first evangelism trip to Daytona Beach. (My Communications professor wasn't too thrilled with the theme of my paper, but feeling like the Lord had just stepped out of the Bible and multiplied loaves and fishes for me made the B- a nonissue.) This trip turned out to be a huge pivoting point in my new Christian life as we shared the gospel with thousands of college students on the beach. The other great thing is that I maintained a relationship with that bank president over the years and even had the chance to meet up with him at a Waffle House in Chattanooga on a road trip to Florida once upon a time. He is now with the Lord, and I think about the investment he made into my life when I was a brand new Christian. I am confident that any fruit that has resulted in my life is also credited to his account in heaven!

The other financial wonder that occurred prior to my crossing-over moment, happened in the middle of my junior year of college. I was a junior at Western Michigan University set to graduate with a degree in Biology in just two more years when I had this crazy idea to change my major to communications (which I sensed was a prompting from the Lord) and to transfer to Boston University (which was a heartfelt desire of mine that I felt had the Lord's approval). Both ideas were rather ridiculous.

Transferring from an in-state public university to an out-of-state private university in the middle of my junior year—while also changing my major—was a moronic thing to consider for these three reasons:

First, I was the assistant director of the dorm complex I lived in and as such, I was receiving free room and board and a small stipend. Didn't make a lot of sense to walk away from that.

Second, transferring from an in-state public school to an out-of-state private university meant my tuition costs at Boston University would more than quadruple! On top of that, my room and board expenses would add thousands more dollars to the crazy situation. It made no financial sense.

Third, transferring schools and changing my major would likely set me back at least a year or more in required credits and courses needed to graduate. By this point, I had taken so many science, math, and biology courses that if I changed my major, there was a good chance that I would not be able to graduate in the four years I had planned but would have to extend my bachelors degree program. Totally not my desire!

All of those nonsensical things made this the perfect opportunity to believe the one thing I knew about God—that with Him, all things are possible! So, I proceeded on a fun faith adventure to do something that seemed ridiculous and exhilarating.

Well, let me cut to the chase and tell you that I did transfer to Boston University in the middle of my junior year. I did change my major. I did graduate with my bachelors degree in just four years.

What happened? God gave me the power to "get wealth" (through large scholarships and grants, a resident advisor job in the dorms and a small student loan) so that I could earn my education, be discipled through Campus Crusade for Christ leaders, graduate with a communications degree, and proceed down the path God had for me. But the biggie? When everything was said and done, it cost me less money out of pocket to transfer to and graduate from Boston University than it would have cost me had I stayed at Western Michigan University. There is no way to explain it other than God's wisdom, favor and goodness.

CROSSING OVER

So this "with God all things are possible" scene was going along pretty well, and I had seen God's hand at work in my finances in practical and powerful ways prior to my crossing-over moment. But then one day, I crossed over. I went from being a taker, to being a giver. #Boom

I was twenty-four years old, a college graduate with a Bachelor of Science in communications from Boston University, and back home in Michigan. That degree landed me the thrilling job of waiting tables at the Harrison Roadhouse Tavern while I tried to figure out the next step.

I had $50 to my name. That's it.

By now I felt God calling me to the ministry to write and teach the Bible for people who knew nothing about God or the Bible, but I had no idea how this was ever going to come to pass. (Mind you, this was a few short decades ago when the options for women in ministry included grand piano player, children's church teacher, or secretary. And that explains why I was waiting tables at a bar.)

Through a series of events, I realized the Lord was leading me to attend a Bible school in Tulsa, Oklahoma, to be trained for ministry and to discover more about His calling on my life. When I did all of the calculations, I figured I needed $2500 for tuition and my first few months of rent. Up until that point, all of my income had gone into my current living expenses, and I had not been able to save any money. Thus one month before Bible school was to begin, I had a grand total of $50 to my name.

One night at church, our pastor taught on the "Prove Me Now" principle of tithes and offerings from Malachi 3. I had never heard such a thing, but I felt faith rising in my heart. When it was time for the offering, I decided to "prove God" according to His Word, and I put all $50 into the offering. (By most standards, it wasn't very much money, but it was all I had. I was soon to learn it's not the amount that God is concerned with. He's looking at the percentage and the motivations of the heart.) I gave that night with the expectation that God would open the windows of heaven over my life and pour out the blessings I needed to go to Bible school. My "Prove Me Now" faith was at the $2500 level because that's what I needed.

You'll never believe what happened. The Tooth Fairy must have picked up a second job because when I woke up the next morning, there was $2500 under my pillow! (Just kidding.) So, what happened? Nothing, at first. But within a few days, a witty idea for a business popped into my heart that I felt was from the Lord. (Now this is where some people say, "Okay, you mentioned something that sounds like work? Uh yeah . . . about that, I'm out.")

As I followed this idea, one thing led to another and within 30 days, I had the $2500 I needed. I moved to Oklahoma to begin training for the ministry. (I'll share more on this later in the book.) What was the secret? I believe several things factored in. I "proved" God according to His Word with faith and a pure heart, and He was faithful to provide me with favor, divine connections, and the innovative power to get wealth—exactly $2500 within that short thirty-day window. And, I worked hard and smart during those 30 days. (News feed notification: Hard work does not kill you.)

Since that time, I have learned many more lessons on wealth and generosity, and my husband and I have seen God's goodness and faithfulness at every level. There is not one magic bullet to lead you to experience a life of wealth and generosity but rather it involves a combination of things like believing God, exercising wisdom, being led by the Spirit, having a strong work ethic, practicing godly stewardship, having pure motives, following witty business ideas, recognizing divine connections, being generous in giving tithes, investing in His Church, sowing offering seeds, and giving alms to the poor. When we respond to God's generosity towards us in these ways, it results in a life of wealth and generosity.

Obviously we cannot give what we do not have, but when we do give what we have, God touches it in remarkable ways. It doesn't matter where you start. We know people who struggle to give $5, but they do it. We know others who are able to give $100,000 on a recurring basis over and above their tithe to build the Church and not even notice the dent in their balance sheet. Your wealth and generosity quotient is probably somewhere in between. Ours is. In our personal lives, we have grown incrementally. Every time God has asked my husband and me to give something—whether it's to start tithing or to give a cup of coffee, a pair of shoes, a car, or big bucks to bless people, build His Church, or help the poor—He has always given us the faith and joy to do so, and He has always been faithful to open the windows of heaven to bless our lives and to multiply the seeds we have sown.

So are you ready to take your own story to the next level?

What am I trying to say? God's promises can be taken to the bank (pun intended). You can trust His Word. You may be like I was as a brand new Christian, a sincere believer with no money, and all of this talk of wealth and generosity may be new and exciting to you. Or you may be a more mature Christian versed in many of these principles, but you've allowed yourself to become rusty when it comes to believing God in the areas of wealth and generosity. No matter where you are in your journey, I pray the Lord uses this book to help you. I pray that you grab onto these principles with a fresh and bold faith to earn more income and to give more money to worthy endeavors than ever before!

Once you cross over into the world of wealth and generosity, there's no desire to go back!

SESSION 1
THE LIFE OF WEALTH
AND GENEROSITY

❧

No need to freak out before we get started. This is not going to be a book about getting Christians to focus all of their time and energy on money. Totally not my goal to perpetuate a self-indulgent, keeping up with the Joneses mentality (and wouldn't ya know, my last name is Jones) or to give people a pie-in-the-sky prosperity gospel view of success and wealth. But it is my goal to help you—yes, you, dear friend—get the basics on what God's Word says about wealth and generosity.

The two go together. True wealth cannot exist apart from a generous spirit. A truly generous lifestyle cannot exist without wealth. (Notification: If you didn't read the "Intro" or "My Story," I highly recommend you go back and do a quick read. It will set you up for this chapter and the rest of the book. Carry on.)

Let me just put it out there. We don't give *to get*. We give because we've already *gotten*. When we give to God in response to the generosity He's already shown us, it turns out that the Lord in His generosity enables us to get more! (Did you follow that?) Second Corinthians 8:9 sums it up nicely, "You know the generous grace of our Lord Jesus Christ. Though he was rich, yet for your sakes he became poor, so that by his poverty he could make you rich."

Do you know that the most generous act in all of time and eternity was when God spared not His own Son, but gave Him up for us all? The Father has already given us His most generous gift by sending His most valued and only begotten Son, Jesus Christ—why wouldn't He generously give us all other things? After all, Romans 8:31-32 tells us, "What then shall we say to these things? If God *is* for us, who *can be* against us? He who did not spare His own Son, but delivered Him up for us all, how shall He not with Him also freely give us all things?" (NKJV). Our response to His generosity is to freely receive all the things we need and then to freely give. That's the best definition of wealth and generosity I know.

I believe we are on the threshold of a wealth and generosity revival among Christians, partly because the devil has worked so hard to hinder believers in their finances and in their ability to be generous. It's time for the tables to turn. As we enforce the enemy's defeat and renew our minds to God's Word and will for our finances, more and more believers will rise up with godly motives, entrepreneurial spirits, and passion to generously support the advancement of the gospel!

We still have a lot of work to do to get the gospel to the ends of the earth, and it's going to take loads of wealth. Thankfully, many wealthy and generous Christians exist. We just need more of them! God has raised up many incredible leaders, Bible teachers, mentors, and coaches who are helping believers understand how to get financial peace by earning more, stewarding, budgeting, and giving like never before. The spirit of generosity has been taking hold in many churches, and believers are tapping into this whole idea of taking God at His Word, favoring His cause, being innovative in the marketplace, stewarding their resources, financing His church, funding gospel initiatives, and helping the poor.

Nevertheless, there are still many in the body of Christ who struggle with this topic, not just theologically, but in practice! What am I saying? Basically this: there are still too many Christians who are flat broke, in debt up to their eyeballs, unable (and often unwilling) to tithe, let alone have anything over and above their tithe to give to gospel work or the poor. On top of that, some believers want to argue about why God wants them poor and unable to give big bucks instead of studying the Bible to get God's heart on what a financially blessed and generous life could look like for them! That's why we need a real, godly revival of wealth and generosity.

You don't need me to tell you. You know that too many Christians are struggling to make ends meet, going from paycheck to credit card to paycheck or working two or three jobs. (You may be one of these people.) The casinos are packed with people, and if you go by the "Honk if You Love Jesus" stickers on the cars in the parking lot, a surprising number of them are Christians trying to hit it big at the black jack table. (And once you—I mean *they*—hit it big, then they'll start tithing. *Wink. Wink.*)

STARTING POINT

Friends, we need to embrace the Father's desire and promise to bless, increase, and prosper His very own children. Without this foundation, we'll always resist, feel guilty, unworthy, or apologetic about success, being blessed, or getting wealth; but without wealth, we cannot be generous!

Wealth and generosity starts with knowing and believing in the love of God: "And we have known and believed the love that God has for us . . ." 1 John 4:16 (NKJV).

Let's start our study by putting things into perspective. While we are going to primarily talk about the practical nuts and bolts of financial wealth and generous giving in this book, the greatest treasure we could ever experience is not measured in dollars and cents, but in knowing and believing in the very real love God the Father, Jesus our Lord and the wonderful Holy Spirit have for us. The truly wealthy person is the one who enjoys a genuine and intimate friendship with the Lord and walks in the wisdom of God's Word.

Let's look at this for a moment as we begin our line-upon-line Bible study.

Philippians 3:8

Yes, everything else is worthless when compared with the infinite value of knowing Christ Jesus my Lord. For his sake I have discarded everything else, counting it all as garbage, so that I could gain Christ.

What is of infinite value? _____

How does everything else (including wealth) compare?_____

_____

Compared to gaining Christ, everything else is counted as what?

_____

Proverbs 3:13-18 (NKJV)

[13]Happy *is* the man *who* finds wisdom, And the man *who* gains understanding; [14] For her proceeds *are* better than the profits of silver, And her gain than fine gold. [15] She *is* more precious than rubies, And all the things you may desire cannot compare with her. [16] Length of days *is* in her right hand, In her left hand riches and honor. [17] Her ways *are* ways of pleasantness, And all her paths *are* peace. [18] She *is* a tree of life to those who take hold of her, And happy *are all* who retain her.

In verses 13 and 18, how would you describe the person who pursues godly wisdom and understanding? _____

_____

In verses 14-16, in what ways is the wealth of wisdom described?

_____

In verse 17, what two words describe wisdom's ways and paths?

_____

3 John 2 (NKJV)

Beloved, I pray that you may prosper in all things and be in health, just as your soul prospers.

What does the Lord, through the apostle John, call us?

_____

What does He desire for us? _____

I like how the *Young's Literal Translation* and the *King James Version* read because it's easy to see the priority of God's desire for His people to prosper when you read the words, "concerning all things" and "above all things." Let's see.

> Beloved, concerning all things I desire thee to prosper, and to be in health, even as thy soul doth prosper. (YLT)

> Beloved, I wish above all things that thou mayest prosper and be in health, even as thy soul prospereth. (KJV)

Notice, He calls us His beloved—His cherished friends—and as such, He wants nothing more than for us to prosper in all things. He wants us to be in health. He wants our soul (our mind, emotions, and will) to prosper. All of these things work together in proportion to one another.

To the degree that our soul is prospering in our relationship with God and in His wisdom, we should experience prosperity and health in all things. Isn't that what any good father wants for his children? Isn't that what any good person desires for his cherished friends?

When I put all of these 3 John 2 translations together in my heart and mind, here's how I hear it, "Dear cherished friends, there are a lot of things I could wish for you in life, but as I have considered all things, concerning all things, and above all things, this is what I so desire for you—that you may prosper and be in health to the same degree that your soul is prospering in your relationship with Me and My Word."

Do you see that?

You may wonder, "Does God really want everyone to prosper in this life?" Absolutely not! There are some people who should definitely not prosper, as it would be detrimental to their lives in every way. The only people who should not prosper are fools. The Bible is clear on that.

Proverbs 1:32 (KJV)

. . . the prosperity of fools shall destroy them.

What happens if a fool prospers? _____

Fools should not prosper because it will indeed destroy them. Fools do not have the wisdom, discipline, or generous spirit that is needed to steward their wealth or their hearts to be generous. So assuming someone is not a fool, the answer to the original question, "Does God really want everyone to prosper in this life?" is, Yes! If their souls are prospering, God wants them to be in health and to prosper!

WHY ARE WEALTH AND GENEROSITY SO ESSENTIAL?

Now that our foundation is set, let's talk about the very practical topics of wealth and generosity. Are you beginning to get the idea that God wants His people to latch onto Him and His plan for their wealth and generosity?

You may wonder why. Why are wealth and generosity essential? Listen to what the Lord told His people in Deuteronomy.

Deuteronomy 8:18 (NKJV)

And you shall remember the LORD your God, for *it is* He who gives you power to get wealth, that He may establish His covenant which He swore to your fathers, as *it is* this day.

Who gives us the power to get wealth? _____

Why does He give us the power to get wealth? _____

_____

God wants to help us "get wealth, that He may establish His covenant." He wants to establish His covenant of mercy, grace, favor, goodness, and blessings both *to* us and *through* us! He wants us to be blessed and to be a blessing. He wants His wealth to come *to* us and to flow *through* us. He wants His people wealthy and generous. He always has!

Think about what it would look like for boatloads of kingdom-minded Christians to have their needs met, to be wealthy, enjoying life, and living in the black. Not only that, imagine these same Christians with generous spirits just dropping by their local churches to say, "Hey Pastor, we've been tithing, sowing and giving, and flowing in God's economy, and the windows of heaven are open so wide. I've got multiple businesses succeeding and more money than I know what to do with. Our family has everything we need, so I just wanted to stop by to pay off the remaining balance on our church building so we could go ahead and get started remodeling the youth center to reach more teens, or go ahead and hire the Kid's Pastor we've been needing. And, while we're at it, why don't we send all of our missionaries an extra $10,000 this week? Here's a check for $800,000. Have a nice day."

I know that sounds over the top for some of you. Truthfully, most pastors would be thrilled to have the Jack and Jill's of their churches stopping by to say, "Hey Pastor, guess what? We've been reading our Bibles and we've decided to get serious about our faith. Starting this Sunday, we're going to begin tithing, and on top of that, we're making a $25 a month pledge to help the new outreach to orphans in Nepal.

Peace." (After local pastors were resuscitated, churches could get some serious kingdom work done!)

It's definitely high time, wouldn't you say, for large numbers of believers to step into a new jet stream and embrace wealth and generosity. When that happens, watch out world!

The generation of Millenials (and the upcoming Generation Z) have a huge heart for justice and benevolent causes, and they are willing to pack up and go to all parts of the world to love and help people in need—whether it's digging water wells, helping widows start micro-businesses, loving orphans, giving dignity to those rescued from the sex-traffic industry, or taking the gospel to the unreached peoples of the earth. They are ready to change the world, and it's going to take big money to fund these efforts.

The Baby Boomers and Gen X'ers don't plan to be left out. They are seasoned, experienced, and more than willing to plant churches and start gospel outposts around the world. In order to pioneer and sustain all of these loving gospel efforts on a continual global scale, it takes money—a lot more cash, dough, Benjamins, moola, greenbacks, bitcoins, and gold bars!

I know I sound like a broken record, but all of this means Christians absolutely must get the basics on wealth and generosity! (And all the people said, "A-to-the-men!")

WEALTH AND GENEROSITY 101

Let's define our terms. What is God's definition of wealth? What is His definition of generosity? How does the Bible depict a financially blessed and generous life? Let's look at several passages that help us understand God's definition of wealth and generosity.

1 Timothy 6:17-19 (NKJV)

[17] Command those who are rich in this present age not to be haughty, nor to trust in uncertain riches but in the living God, who gives us richly all things to enjoy. [18] *Let them* do good, that they be rich in good works, ready to give, willing to share, [19] storing up for themselves a good foundation for the time to come, that they may lay hold on eternal life.

In verse 17, what does God tell the rich not to do? _____

_____

In verse 17, what does God gives us richly? _____

_____

In verse 18, what does God tell the rich to do? _____

_____

In verse 19, what kind of lasting dividends does wealth provide for those who are generous?_____

_____

So, what does this mean to you?_____

_____

Can you see that the real issue isn't money? The real issue is trust. The Bible teaches that we cannot trust in both God and money; our trust must be in one or the other. God wants us to trust in Him and use money for helping others and enjoying life. We should trust in the living God and recognize that He richly gives us all things for two basic reasons:

1) To enjoy life!

2) To be generous!

How does that translate into our lives? For many people it's a shift in thinking. You begin to think like a wealthy and generous person. For instance, you see yourself as valuable and worthy of being blessed as well as capable of being a blessing. You get rid of the pauper mindset and see yourself as the beloved royal son or daughter of the King that you are. You get rid of the "mine, mine, mine" or "hoard, hoard, hoard" mindset and see yourself as a blessed "give, give, give" person.

Think about it.

When it comes to *enjoying life*, the Lord wants you to know it is God, who gives us richly all things to enjoy, so you can quit apologizing or feeling guilty for being blessed—and while we're on this topic, make sure you don't judge other believers who are living the dream. Just accept the fact that God loves you and wants you blessed and enjoying life (and giving, but we'll get to that in a minute). That means it's time to stop thinking like Secondhand Sue. (It's not that you can't still love a great sale or shopping at thrift stores, it's just that you quit thinking like a second-class citizen.) When you realize God wants to bless you richly so you enjoy life, you'll start to believe that your path will shine brighter and brighter. You'll be thankful for His abundant favor and goodness.

Do you know how often God—in various ways and through various people in the Bible—asked His people: "What do you want?" (Notice, He never asks: "Will this do?" "Would you settle for this?" "Do you like this liquidated item?") Don't get me wrong, there is nothing wrong with a good deal, but sometimes you just have to be okay with enjoying God's goodness, even if it's not on clearance! Go ahead and order your steak with the blue cheese upgrade. Get the hash browns for an extra $1.69. Upgrade your seats on a flight, take a vacation with your family, buy the boat, or join a club. Give yourself permission to enjoy life!

When it comes to *giving*, because of God's generosity towards you, your automatic response should be to give! The Lord wants this to be our default. "Let them do good, that they be rich in good works, ready to give, willing to share" (1 Timothy 6:18 NKJV). When you live to give, it causes you to listen to what people desire, and then one of your first thoughts is: *How can I make that happen for them?* You think about picking up the tab at lunch, buying coffees for the office, paying down someone's mortgage, sending a family on an all-expenses paid vacation, funding things at your church, supporting missionaries, sponsoring children in underprivileged countries, and more.

Are you beginning to catch the spirit of wealth and generosity?

I know the definition for wealth and generosity may vary from person to person. For some, the definition of being blessed might be having the means to *buy* a Mercedes G class. For others, a blessed life is the ability to *give* a Mercedes G class. For another, it's both!

As I mentioned in "My Story," there was a season where being able to buy Del Monte canned pineapple instead of the generic brand would have been the epitome of a blessed life. Let's look at the sliding scale of a blessed and generous life.

Maybe a financially successful life for one person is the ability to move from his two bedroom, double-wide mobile home into a two-story house with four bedrooms; for another, it's having the means to pay off his neighbor's mortgage. For one person, being wealthy is having the ability to clothe his kids; for another, it's the ability to put all of his kids in orthodontic braces. For one person, being wealthy is having the ability to sponsor a child in an underprivileged nation; for another, it's being the kid who is sponsored. A swimming pool with water is a blessed life in America; having water to drink is a blessed life in remote villages in Africa. A wealthy and generous life for an American in Beverly Hills is going to look a lot different than the blessed life for someone living in Calcutta, India. We need to realize that the reality of poverty does not negate God's blessing, nor should it cause those who experience the reality of God's blessings to feel guilty or ashamed. Rather, both of these realities should inspire us to experience the reality of wealth and success so that we can ease the burden of poverty on those in our sphere of influence.

God's Word is clear on His definition of wealth and generosity. He's not confused at all. We get confused when we measure God's standard against our own experience of these things. If we are not careful, we will allow the experiences we have had personally or the things we see on the news to become our standard for God's will. Does that make sense? In other words, we should always allow God's Word to define His will, and then as we believe His Word, our experience will come up to that standard rather than bring God's will down to the standard of our experience.

We have traveled to many parts of the world to minister God's Word and have seen extreme prosperity in places like Singapore and Monaco and extreme squalor in places like Haiti and Mexico. If we just go by what our eyes see, we might think it's God's will for some places to be blessed with abundance and other places to be cursed with poverty. We know that's not true because if you drive a few short miles in any direction in either of those countries, you will see areas of need in Singapore and Monaco. (Although since the entire country of Monaco is only 499 acres large, which is three-fourths of a square mile in size, and is known as the "richest place on earth," you won't see too much poverty there!) If you drive a few miles in Haiti or Mexico, you'll find the "rich neighborhoods" where people are living the life. Rich and poor alike are in every nation.

If you've seen an H&M clothing store, Apple store, or a Rolex store in New York City or Shanghai, there's one just like it in London or Rome. They're all the same. If you've seen street vendors selling fake watches or purses in Athens or Istanbul, the same thing is in Bangkok and San Francisco. The rich and the poor are active in every city—often just blocks from one another. In cities around the world, you'll see the homeless eat pizza crusts out of a trash bin and beg on the streets while in that same city, the wealthy eat pizza by the pool and play golf at twilight.

People are people. Only the faces, languages, and hair colors change! Wealth and poverty, greed and generosity are not city or nation specific. But thankfully, God has leveled the playing field for everyone everywhere by giving us His Word. Faith in God and His Word *is* the secret sauce that brings real change to individuals, families, communities, and nations when it comes to wealth and generosity.

What do I mean?

Financially, everyone everywhere starts somewhere. Whether you start with ten cents, ten dollars, or ten rupees, if you begin to cooperate with God's principles for wealth and generosity, the only way you can go is up! The playing field is level in that respect. Granted, a Christian in America (where the GDP is around $53,000) is more likely to start with 200 dollars than a believer in Burundi (where the GDP is around $260) who might start with 98 cents. But either way, by applying God's principles through faith and patience, the only way to go is up! The bottom line is simple. If we want to go up in the areas of wealth and generosity, we will have to grow up in our understanding. If we want to experience abundant living, we have to embrace generous giving.

So let's move on and talk about money.

MONEY, MONEY, MONEY

How should a believer think, view, or feel about money? Does God want Christians to hate money as evil, avoid money, or choose between God and money? As we will discover, money is not evil. Money is neutral; the love of money is what creates the evil. In the hands of a loving, generous person, money can do great good. In the hands of a selfish, evil person, money can bring great harm. God doesn't want our trust or love to be in money. He wants our affection to be set on Him. When we trust God, we can have money. When we trust in money, we can't have God. (We'll talk more about that in our future sessions.) Let's start with some basic understanding of what the Bible says about money.

Matthew 6:24 (NIV)

No one can serve two masters. Either you will hate one and love the other or you will be devoted to one and despise the other. You cannot serve both God and money.

No one can serve what? _____

We will _____ one and _____ the other.

We will be _____ to one and _____ the other.

We cannot serve what? _____ and _____.

It's true. Jesus says we cannot serve both God and money. But what did He mean by this? Did He mean you can't serve God and have money? Did He mean if you have money you can't serve God? What does it mean to serve money?

When we serve money, we allow it to tell us what we can do, not do, give, and not give. When money is the boss of us, it makes us a slave. When we serve God, we allow Him to tell us what we can do, not do, give, and not give. This is much more liberating—especially since He is the source of everything we have, including money.

Proverbs 11:28

Trust in your money and down you go! But the godly flourish like leaves in spring.

What happens if you trust in your money?_____

What happens to the godly? _____

1 Timothy 6:10

For the love of money is the root of all kinds of evil. And some people, craving money, have wandered from the true faith and pierced themselves with many sorrows.

Is money or the love of money the root of all kinds of evil?

_____

Again, it's the love and craving for money that is the root of all evil. Money itself is neutral. If we maintain the right perspective and relationship with money, it can be a powerful tool for good and for getting the gospel to the world, for building churches, for helping

Christian organizations and for helping the poor and needy receive help and justice.

Psalm 112:5

Good comes to those who lend money generously and conduct their business fairly.

What happens to the generous and fair? _____

Psalm 15:5

Those who lend money without charging interest, and who cannot be bribed to lie about the innocent. Such people will stand firm forever.

What happens to those who are generous to lend money without interest? _____

Hebrews 13:5

Don't love money; be satisfied with what you have. For God has said, "I will never fail you. I will never abandon you."

What are we not to love? _____

What does contentment look like according to this verse?_____

_____

When we have the Lord in our lives, we have more than any amount of money could ever buy. While God wants us to be content with what we have, He is the same God who gives us many promises concerning His desire to give us the power to get wealth and to be generous.

Now that we've discussed our definitions, realities, motivations, trust, and love when it comes to wealth and generosity, let's get established in the fact that when our hearts are in the right place, God indeed does want His children to get wealth.

12 PROOFS GOD WANTS HIS PEOPLE TO GET WEALTH

Let's start with the most basic question: How do we know God wants His people to get wealth? Let's look at twelve Bible words that define God's will around this topic: wealth, prosperity, prosper, rich, profit, abundantly, increase, fruitful, multiply, substance, treasures, and success.

1. Wealth

The Hebrew word for "wealth" is *chayil*.[1] Its meaning includes a force, wealth, riches, strength, army, and substance.

Deuteronomy 8:18 (NKJV)

And you shall remember the LORD your God, for *it is* He who gives you power to get wealth, that He may establish His covenant which He swore to your fathers, as *it is* this day.

We've looked at this verse before, but since God literally uses the phrase, "it is He who gives you power to *get wealth*," that should settle the fact that He wants you to get wealth. The End.

Let's study it out a bit more.

What does God give us the power to get? _____

_____

How do you define wealth? _____

_____

What is the purpose for this wealth? _____

What are we to remember? (Hint: See verse 18.) _____

_____

Notice, God is the one who gives us the power to "get wealth." It must be okay with Him for His people to get wealth! He has reasons for wanting us to get wealth, as we will see in our study. He's not keeping or prohibiting His people from getting wealth. He wants us to get wealth for a reason. From this passage, it's easy to see that a primary purpose for getting wealth is to establish His covenant to us and through us.

Psalm 66:12 (KJV)

We went through fire and through water: but thou broughtest us out into a wealthy place.

I like how the *Amplified Bible* phrases this verse, "we went through fire and through water, but You brought us out into a broad, moist place [to abundance and refreshment and the open air]."

After we've been through a difficult time, what is possible? _____

_____

How would you describe a wealthy place? _____

_____

We all go through rough patches in life and in our finances due to our own poor choices and because of the choices of others. God's desire is to bring us through the fire and water into a wealthy place, a place of strength, increase, and wealth where we are a force to be reckoned with—wealthy in spirit, soul, body, relationally, and financially.

Proverbs 3:9

Honor the LORD with your wealth and with the best part of everything you produce.

What are we to do with our wealth? _____

2. Prosperity

The Hebrew word for "prosperity" is *shalom*.[2] Its meaning includes safety, welfare, health, prosperity, peace, and rest. We can see that God's definition of prosperity is all-encompassing!

Psalm 35:27 (NKJV)

Let them shout for joy and be glad, who favor my righteous cause; and let them say continually, "Let the LORD be magnified, who has pleasure in the prosperity of His servant."

What gives the Lord pleasure?_____

Who does God want to prosper? _____

What are we supposed to say continually? _____

Are you a servant of God? _____

According to this verse, would it please God to see you prosper?

_____

What does the first part of the verse tell you to do? _____

_____

Take a moment to picture God delighting in your prosperity. Have you ever imagined that your prosperity blesses Him?

_____

From a parental point of view, why do you think God wants His children to prosper? _____

3. Prosper

The Greek word for "prosper" is *euodoo*.[3] Its meaning includes to succeed in reaching, to succeed in business affairs, a prosperous journey, to cause to prosper, and to be successful.

3 John 2 (NKJV)

Beloved, I pray that you may prosper in all things and be in health, just as your soul prospers.

What does the Holy Spirit, through the apostle John, tell us God desires above all things? _____

_____

What type of prosperity is He describing? _____

_____

Our prosperity and our health are supposed to be in proportion to what? _____

Is your soul prospering?_____

If your soul (mind, emotions, and will) is not prospering, you may need to spend some time focusing on this area, specifically to get your mind renewed to God's Word, to get your emotions and will under the control of the Word and the Holy Spirit. This is such an important area because when our souls are not healthy or prospering, it often affects our physical health as well as our success in life. I encourage you to seek some help if you need it.

4. Rich

The Hebrew word for "rich" is *ashar*.[4] Its meaning includes to accumulate, to make self-rich, to grow rich.

Proverbs 10:22 (NKJV)

The blessing of the LORD makes *one* rich, and He adds no sorrow with it.

What does the blessing of the Lord do in your life? _____

_____

According to the definition of "rich," as described above, how would you describe "makes one rich"? _____

_____

What does "he adds no sorrow with it" mean? _____

_____

In your own words, how would you describe being rich with no sorrow? _____

Obviously, it's possible to become rich without the Lord. Many people who don't know or honor the Lord are rich and live big lives on private islands with personal chefs. (Not that any of us wouldn't welcome those things. But seriously.) The problem is that having a boatload of bucks and a fleet of Brinks trucks to haul it around is not enough. Without the Lord, riches have been the ruin of people. Often those kinds of riches bring the sorrows of being a workaholic, not knowing who your real friends are, having to hide your addiction to prescription drugs, enduring a shallow or unhappy marriage, being estranged from your kids, and dealing with health issues. Living in the fast, rich lane has a way of stealing people's peace of mind, their joy of living, and can even result in premature death. That, my friend, is not the plan. On top of that, it's all so very temporary and has no eternal value. When we do things God's way, the Bible promises that He makes us rich and adds no sorrow with it, and our wealth and generosity not only provide temporary blessings, but also produce eternal fruit.

Ecclesiastes 5:19 (NKJV)

As for every man to whom God has given riches and wealth, and given him power to eat of it, to receive his heritage and rejoice in his labor—this *is* the gift of God.

What did Solomon describe as the "gift of God"? _____

_____

5. Profit

The Hebrew word for "profit" is *ya'al*.[5] Its meaning includes to ascend, to benefit, and to be valuable.

Isaiah 48:17 (NKJV)

Thus says the LORD, your Redeemer, the Holy One of Israel: "I *am* the LORD your God, Who teaches you to profit, Who leads you by the way you should go."

What two things does your Redeemer say He will do for you?

_____

Do you think God will ever teach you something or lead you in a way that is contrary to His will? _____

If He is going to teach you to profit and lead you in the way you should go, can you conclude that it is His will for you to profit?

_____

_____

6. Abundantly

The Greek word for "abundantly" is *perissos*.[6] Its meaning includes more than is necessary, superadded, extraordinary, surpassing, the sense of beyond, superabundant in quantity or superior in quality, excessive, preeminence, exceedingly abundantly above, more abundantly, beyond measure.

John 10:10 (NKJV)

The thief does not come except to steal, and to kill, and to destroy. I have come that they may have life, and that they may have *it* more abundantly.

What did Jesus say He came to bring? _____

How would you define abundant life? _____

_____

If you are in poverty and lack, are you in the abundant life?

_____

Do you get the idea from these definitions that God's will for His children in the area of wealth, prosperity, abundance, and blessings includes something above and beyond average?

_____

_____

And, how good are these two versions of John 10:10 from the *Message Bible* and *Amplified Bible*?

I came so they can have real and eternal life, more and better life than they ever dreamed of. (MSG)

The thief comes only in order to steal and kill and destroy. I came that they may have and enjoy life, *and* have it in abundance (to the full, till it overflows). (AMPC)

Romans 8:32 (NKJV)

He who did not spare His own Son, but delivered Him up for us all, how shall He not with Him also freely give us all things?

What is the most precious gift God ever gave to mankind?

_____

What else does God say He will give us?_____

_____

What can "all things" include? _____

_____

Ephesians 3:20 (NKJV)

Now to Him who is able to do exceedingly abundantly above all that we ask or think, according to the power that works in us.

What does God want to do? _____

_____

How does God want to bless His people? _____

_____

7. Increase

The Hebrew word for "increase" is _yacaph._[7] It means to add, to increase and to do again, continue, exceed, get more.

Psalm 115:14 (NKJV)

May the LORD give you increase more and more, you and your children.

What will the Lord do for our children and us? _____

_____

In what ways do you need the Lord to increase you and your children? I told you my wild Colter Bay, tent cabin family vacation story in the "My Story" section of this book, but let me redeem myself when it comes to family vacations. It might sound crazy, but I seem to have faith for vacations. (Doesn't everyone?) The thing is, when our kids were little and we were living on a shoestring budget and pioneering a church, I really had a desire for our family to experience an annual vacation to build lifelong memories for our kids. Since we were in God's economic flow, He seemed to bring all kinds of fun vacation deals our way, and as a result, we took some of the coolest family vacations every year while our kids were school age. Honestly, even still, the Lord puts incredible vacation deals in front us on a regular basis. (He wants to do the same for you!)

One crazy story has to do with a timeshare purchase when an email randomly popped into my inbox from a timeshare auction company. I just happened to scroll through this email to see if there were any good deals on timeshares at ski resorts in Colorado. While scrolling, I saw a timeshare for sale in Palm Springs. We had never been to Palm Springs, but this timeshare caught my attention because it was in a gated community and for sale for only $500. I thought it was a typo. I forwarded the link to my husband and jokingly said, "Hey, what do you think about buying a time share in Palm Springs?" I totally forgot about it, and two weeks later while I was out of town, he called me and said, "Congratulations! We bought a timeshare in Palm Springs!"

I couldn't believe it. I told him I was just kidding. He said, "Well, kidding or not, we own a timeshare!" Ok, so here's the craziest part. He didn't buy it for $500; he bought it for $250! Yes, half the asking price! The backstory is this: two sisters owned several timeshare units and they just wanted to reduce their overhead. They were both attorneys, and when my husband offered them $250 instead of the $500 they were asking, they accepted his offer and filed all the paper work for free! As it turns out, our timeshare is in a beautiful little complex in Indian Wells right next to the mountains. (This is one of the wealthiest parts of Palm Springs that Lucille Ball and Desi Arnez made famous!) We've owned it for over 10 years now and our annual trek to Palm Springs' hot, dry, sunny, blue-sky desert scenery is one of the highlights of our year! #boomboom

That's God's increase! So what are the desires of your heart in these areas?

8. Multiply

The Hebrew word for "multiply" is *rabah*.[8] The same word is translated as abundance and increase. Its meaning includes to increase in whatever respect, bring in abundance, enlarge, exceedingly, be full of, heap, multiply, plenty.

Genesis 1:27-28 (NKJV)

So God created man in His *own* image; in the image of God He created him; male and female He created them. [28] Then God blessed them, and God said to them, "Be fruitful and multiply;

fill the earth and subdue it; have dominion over the fish of the sea, over the birds of the air, and over every living thing that moves on the earth."

What are the first four words God ever spoke to man? He could have said anything; what did He say? _____

_____

The words "fruitful" and "multiply" are coupled together in many passages of Scripture, and it's easy to see that God's idea of being fruitful and multiplying includes more than bearing generations of children.

The very first words God spoke to man were words of wealth! By definition alone, it's easy to see that God wants His children to increase in every respect, to bring things into abundance, to enlarge exceedingly, to be full of all kinds of things, to multiply in heaps, and to have plenty! Do you get any sense that the Lord wants His people to experience lack, decrease, barely making ends meet, or poverty in any way?

9. Fruitful

The Greek word for "fruitful" is *karpophoreo*.[9] It means to bear fruit, bring forth fruit, be fruitful.

Colossians 1:9-10 (NKJV)

For this reason we also, since the day we heard it, do not cease to pray for you, and to ask that you may be filled with the knowledge of His will in all wisdom and spiritual understanding; [10] that you may walk worthy of the Lord, fully pleasing *Him*, being fruitful in every good work and increasing in the knowledge of God.

What does God want believers to do?_____

_____

_____

In other words, there's nothing that sounds like lack, barrenness, or poverty in the word "fruitful." Because we are in Christ, as we are filled with the knowledge of God and His will, we are expected to bring forth fruit—spirit, soul and body!

10. Substance

There are two Hebrew words we want to look at. One is *rekush*, which means property, goods, riches, substance.[10] The other is *yesh*, which means being, existence, substance.[11]

This is a good word! Substance is talking about material things.

2 Chronicles 32:27-30 (NKJV)

Hezekiah had very great riches and honor. And he made himself treasuries for silver, for gold, for precious stones, for spices, for shields, and for all kinds of desirable items; [28] storehouses for the harvest of grain, wine, and oil; and stalls for all kinds of livestock, and folds for flocks. [29] Moreover he provided cities for himself, and possessions of flocks and herds in abundance; for God had given him very much property. [30] This same Hezekiah also stopped the water outlet of Upper Gihon, and brought the water by tunnel to the west side of the City of David. Hezekiah prospered in all his works.

Hezekiah, another of God's servants, was quite rich. How do these verses describe God's blessing in his life?_____

_____

Who gave him his "substance"? _____

Luke 8:1-3 (NKJV)

Now it came to pass, afterward, that He went through every city and village, preaching and bringing the glad tidings of the kingdom of God. And the twelve were with Him, ² and certain women who had been healed of evil spirits and infirmities— Mary called Magdalene, out of whom had come seven demons, ³ and Joanna the wife of Chuza, Herod's steward, and Susanna, and many others who provided for Him from their substance.

What did these believing women—Joanna, Susanna, and many others—minister to (or honor) Jesus with? _____

_____

Can you see that God wants us to be blessed with "substance"— things that will be a blessing to us and with which we can honor Him?

11. Treasures

The Hebrew word for "treasures" is *owtsar*.[12] It means treasure, store-house, treasure house, and depository.

Proverbs 8:21 (NKJV)

That I may cause those who love me to inherit wealth, that I may fill their treasuries.

If we seek wisdom, what will happen to our treasures?

_____

Proverbs 15:6 (NKJV)

In the house of the righteous *there* is much treasure, but in the revenue of the wicked is trouble.

What is in the house of the righteous? _____

Proverbs 21:20 (NKJV)

There is desirable treasure, and oil in the dwelling of the wise, but a foolish man squanders it.

What is in the dwelling of the wise? _____

Treasures are the by-product of God's wisdom and His blessing in our lives.

12. Success

The Hebrew word for "success" is *sakal*.[13] It means to be prudent, be circumspect, wisely understand, prosper.

Joshua 1:8 (NKJV)

This Book of the Law shall not depart from your mouth, but you shall meditate in it day and night, that you may observe to do according to all that is written in it. For then you will make your way prosperous, and then you will have good success.

If we want to have prosperity and good success in our lives, what does God tell us to do?_____

_____

Notice a key phrase in this passage, "you will make your way prosperous, and then you will have good success." This is huge because sometimes people get the idea that God will just make it rain money when they seek Him. Sometimes Christians think the ball is in God's court and they are passively waiting for blessings and success. Nothing could be further from the truth. He gives us the power to get wealth, to make our way prosperous. This means a strong work ethic, the spirit of wisdom, intentional innovation, and a burst of entrepreneurialism need a big time revival among God's people.

Whether you're an empty nester thinking about how you want to invest the second half of your life or you're in the middle of your career and an expert at management, investing, flipping real estate, buying businesses, or wheeling, dealing, and multiplying your wealth—God has more for you! Maybe you're a young entrepreneur just starting out and tapping into the Internet and global markets that give you unprecedented opportunities for success and wealth. Whatever your current situation, God wants to help you make your way prosperous!

Let me tell you a few stories about the creativity of Millennials.

You probably know that Mark Zuckerberg was a sophomore at Harvard when he co-founded Facebook (at the present time, valued at around $250 billion)! It was three college students from Helsinki University of Technology (now called Aalto University School of Science) who developed what we know as Angry Birds, one of the most downloaded app games of all time. Ever heard of Google? Larry Page was 22 years old and Sergey Brin was 21 when they met at Stanford and, a few years later, created Google. All of these folks were in their twenties when they attempted great things—like trying to take over the world. They became multi-billionaires and generous philanthropists with great influence. I wonder what the Lord could do to change the world, build His Church, and connect more people to Jesus through a group of smart, dedicated, eternity-minded, church-loving, Jesus-focused, generous Millenials? Like, you! (Mmmm, why don't you let us know?)

Anna is a young lady we know who didn't start a social media behemoth, but she did find success in the scarf niche. She has a great eye for fabrics and began making and selling "limited editions" of her eternity scarves on Etsy. Her reputation and the demand for her scarves became so great, she sold out of her scarves before a new release even went on sale publically! Etsy and all of the other fabulous online classified, selling, or aution sites are a gift to this generation of entreprenuers. Did you know that the current top seller on Etsy is Bohemian Findings with annual sales of $448,192? They sell charms and other small items. Are your wheels starting to spin?

Ben and Tori are a young married couple in our church, taking their cues from Chip and Joanna Gaines' popular reality show, *Fixer Upper*. He's a builder, and she has a good eye for design. Together they are buying fixer uppers and transforming them into beautiful homes they sell for a nice profit.

A friend, whose daughter went to Oxford in England, told us about two Oxford men who needed some extra cash, so they bought a blender, several tubs of ice cream, boxes of candy bars, and gallons of milk and began blending milk shakes for their friends at $2 a cup. This idea took off!

Here's another and I love this one: Insomnia Cookies. This company delivers freshly baked cookies and cold milk to your front door

SESSION 1: THE LIFE OF WEALTH AND GENEROSITY

from noon until 3 a.m.! Insomnia was founded in a dorm room by college student Seth Berkowitz when he was a student at the University of Pennsylvania. Now Insomnia Cookies has over 85 other branches. We have a branch in Kalamazoo, and I know how popular they are with the college kids who keep them busy until the wee hours of the night—especially during exams!

What genius idea does God want to drop into your lap?

If you're a parent or pastor of Millennials, let me encourage you. I know you want your kids to get hold of God's plan for their success, wealth, and generosity, just as we desired those things for our kids. While all four of our kids felt God's call to ministry and are dedicated to using their gifts to build His Church, we've also done our best to teach them how to believe God for witty, entrepreneurial ideas where their talents could be monetized for extra streams of income. We often reminded them of the four "Rs" to accumulating wealth: rentals, residuals, royalties, and real estate. The result is that each of them (and their spouses!) have begun the journey and found part-time innovative niches where they can "get wealth."

Our oldest daughter, Meghan, leads our creative department and is fully immersed in ministry, but a few years ago, she found out about Poshmark, a popular website for selling clothing. She began to sell clothes from her own closet that were in good condition and in a short time, she established herself as a quality top seller. At the time of this writing, she has over 150,000 followers. Our son-in-law, Brodie, heads up our Media Tech and Bible School Ministry which keeps him busy. From the time he was in high school, he's been using his entrepreneurial mind to find, buy, and sell all kind of eclectic, liquidated items on eBay and Craig's List. The result for Meghan and Brodie has been tens of thousands of dollars in extra income to enjoy life, take trips, and give generously.

Similar stories could be told of our other kids. Our daughter Annie serves as our high school ministry director and in the evenings or on Saturdays, she has made extra income using her experience playing high school and college volleyball to pick up part time volleyball coaching jobs. Our son Luke led our worship department and our daughter-in-law Kelsey served in our communications ministry before they moved to Australia for Bible college. Prior to their move, in their spare time, they were earning several extra streams of income by using their creative design skills to do freelance graphic work for others as well as using their photography skills for weddings and senior pictures. Our youngest son Eric serves in our high school and video ministries. In his spare time, he started a media company where he makes customized videos for businesses. His passion is ministry, but God has blessed his video business, and it is thriving.

I hope all of these examples have encouraged you. There is no doubt; the Lord has innovative, entrepreneurial ideas for anyone who desires them.

In the few passages we've looked up, can you see that God clearly desires for His children to get wealth? Kingdom minded people of all generations are using their God-given ingenuity, finance and leadership gifts, sales and marketing skills, and creative abilities to established their niche in the world. God is helping them to "make their way prosperous!" So what is your response to all these promises of God? It should be "Yes and Amen!" You don't have to "wonder" if God wants these things for you. He's already told us, "For all the promises of God in Him *are* Yes, and in Him Amen, to the glory of God through us" (2 Corinthians 1:20, NKJV).

12 REASONS SOME PEOPLE WILL NEVER HAVE WEALTH

Let's take a moment to look at the reverse side of wealth and increase; that is, poverty and lack. If God desires for His children to get wealth and to be generous, why does it seem like some people never prosper or get ahead? We can learn a lot about what something *is* by looking at what it *is not.* Let's look at twelve reasons some people will never have wealth.

1. Lack of Seeking the Lord

Hosea 4:6 (NIV)

My people are destroyed for lack of knowledge . . .

What causes God's people to be destroyed? _____

_____

When we don't know the things we don't know, destruction can wreak havoc in areas of our lives. Turns out, ignorance is not bliss. When we don't know what God wants for our lives, we can't access it and in fact, we might experience things that are contrary to it and not even know it. For example, if I don't know God desires for me to prosper and be in good health even as my soul prospers, then when things that are contrary to prosperity come knocking on my door, I may think God sent those destructive things to teach me a lesson and rather than resisting them, I might inadvertently welcome them into my life. That's why it's so important to obtain the knowledge of God and His will and His Word. (Bravo to you for doing just that!)

Psalm 34:10 (NKJV)

The young lions lack and suffer hunger; but those who seek the LORD shall not lack any good thing.

What will those who seek the Lord not lack? _____

_____

2. Dishonesty

Proverbs 13:11 (NKJV)

Wealth *gained* by dishonesty will be diminished, but he who gathers by labor will increase.

Wealth gotten by dishonesty does what? _____

Wealth gotten by labor does what?_____

Ephesians 4:28

If you are a thief, quit stealing. Instead, use your hands for good hard work, and then give generously to others in need.

God doesn't want us to steal things. What does He want us to do?

_____

What does the Lord want us to do with the wages we earn?

_____

3. No Initiative

Proverbs 6:6-11 (NKJV)

Go to the ant, you sluggard! Consider her ways and be wise,[7] which, having no captain, overseer or ruler, [8]provides her supplies in the summer, *and* gathers her food in the harvest. [9]How long will you slumber, O sluggard? When will you rise from your sleep? [10]A little sleep, a little slumber, a little folding of the hands to sleep—[11] so shall your poverty come on you like a prowler, and your need like an armed man.

What can we learn from the ant? _____

_____

What happens to the sluggard?_____

_____

Poverty comes upon those who do what? _____

_____

What role and responsibility do we have for taking the initiative in our own success? _____

_____

2 Thessalonians 3:10

Even while we were with you, we gave you this command: "Those unwilling to work will not get to eat."

We have a responsibility to work and to be a good steward of our financial resources.

Who doesn't get to eat? _____

4. Loves Sleep

Proverbs 20:13

If you love sleep, you will end in poverty. Keep your eyes open, and there will be plenty to eat!

What is the cause of poverty in these passages? _____

_____

5. Stingy

Proverbs 11:24

Give freely and become more wealthy; be stingy and lose everything.

What is the cause of poverty in this scripture? _____

What results for the giving person? _____

6. Unteachable

Proverbs 13:18

If you ignore criticism, you will end in poverty and disgrace; if you accept correction, you will be honored.

According to this verse, what causes poverty? _____

_____

7. Wrong Friends

Proverbs 23:19-21

My child, listen and be wise: Keep your heart on the right course. Do not carouse with drunkards or feast with gluttons, for they are on their way to poverty, and too much sleep clothes them in rags.

What three things cause a person to be in poverty?

_____

_____

8. No Common Sense

Proverbs 24:30-34

I walked by the field of a lazy person, the vineyard of one with no common sense. I saw that it was overgrown with nettles. It was covered with weeds, and its walls were broken down. Then, as I looked and thought about it, I learned this lesson: A little extra sleep, a little more slumber, a little folding of the hands to rest—then poverty will pounce on you like a bandit; scarcity will attack you like an armed robber.

What is the cause of poverty in this passage? _____

In your own words, describe the missing elements in this person's work ethic. _____

_____

9. Chases Fantasies

Proverbs 28:19

A hard worker has plenty of food, but a person who chases fantasies ends up in poverty.

What type of person shall have plenty? _____

What type of person shall have poverty? _____

Do you know dreamers? Dreams are great! Dreams give us hope. Dreams can be great blueprints for a desired future. But dreamers who are always dreaming and never working hard to execute those dreams are just chasing fantasies and will end up in poverty. So what's the moral of that story? Wake. Up. Dreamer. Work. Smart. And. Work. Hard.

10. Lazy

Proverbs 10:4

Lazy people are soon poor; hard workers get rich.

Who becomes poor? _____

Who gets rich? _____

11. Trapped in a Cycle of Poverty

Proverbs 10:15

The wealth of the rich is their fortress; the poverty of the poor is their destruction.

Sometimes people get trapped in a cycle of poverty, and it's passed from one generation to another.

What destroys the poor? _____

Thankfully, God's principles for wealth and generosity can lift the poor out of their destruction.

12. Unfaithful

Luke 16:10-12

If you are faithful in little things, you will be faithful in large ones. But if you are dishonest in little things, you won't be honest with greater responsibilities.[11] And if you are untrustworthy about worldly wealth, who will trust you with the true riches of heaven? [12] And if you are not faithful with other people's things, why should you be trusted with things of your own?

It takes faith to be faithful! We have to work hard in the little things in order to be entrusted with bigger things.

If we are faithful in little things, what happens? _____

_____

If we are dishonest in little things, what is the result? _____

_____

If we are untrustworthy about worldly wealth, what can we not be
trusted with? _____

If we are not faithful with other people's things, what is the result?

_____

It is evident from these passages that lack, poverty, and being poor
are not God's will or desire for His children. Can you see it? You could
say it takes more faith to get wealth than it does to become poor. It
takes more faith to live as a giver than it does to live a stingy life. It's
easy to go nowhere and give nothing. It's not recommended, but it's
easy to do. God has something better for His kids. He wants us to get
wealth and give generously.

So, let's crush that poor, stingy, barely get by, second-hand, poverty
mindset and let's live in God's economy! Let's summarize what we've
studied so far by looking at the type of mindset we should have when
it comes to our own wealth and generosity.

OUR MINDSET WHEN IT COMES
TO WEALTH AND GENEROSITY

It seems like there are two extremes among many Christians.

One extreme is the poverty mindset. The idea here is that God
does not want Christians to be wealthy or prosperous because it is
more spiritual and noble to be poor. Hopefully by now you've seen
enough Scripture to know this isn't so. Believers with this mindset do
everything in their power to avoid earning, saving, or investing money

for fear of becoming covetous and materialistic. Generally, believers with this view do not tithe or give generously; instead, they are on the receiving end of others' generosity.

The other extreme is the eccentric prosperity mentality. The idea here is that God wants Christians to focus on wealth and material things as an indicator of God's blessings in their lives, to the exclusion of generosity and godly stewardship. Believers with this view are often out of balance, workaholics, prideful, and stingy with their blessings.

Both of these extremes are dangerous. The "noble," poverty-minded extreme creates poor Christians who cannot support themselves, let alone give generously. The eccentric prosperity-minded extreme creates selfish Christians who won't give generously because they idolize their materialistic lifestyle.

God wants us to have an honest, truthful, moral, and Biblical view when it comes to this topic. In his classic book, *God's Plan for Man,* Finis Jennings Dake gave one of the most intelligent, direct, and exhortative pieces of advice when he wrote this:

"If it is God's will and Word for man to have all the good things of life, then man is under moral obligation to seek to attain to the known will of God to get these things. When he is passive, indifferent, and faithless he is sinning against moral law and moral government, and he is not living up to his moral obligation to get these benefits so that he can be a good and perfect example to other moral agents.

"It is the height of folly to think that man is living up to his moral obligation, that he is the best example to other moral agents, that he has faith and is obedient to God, and that he is securing the best good to his being as well as to all others, when he is . . . helpless, unhappy, and poverty stricken. Yet Christians by the multitudes think and are being taught to be satisfied with this lot in life, to endure patiently these limitations, to accept these evils as the will of God, and to make no effort to get out of these conditions in life. They actually think that they can best glorify God and be a Christian example by being willing to endure these sufferings as they say, for Christ's sake.

"If they really could see that they are enduring evils for the sake of the false doctrines of men, they would know that they are submitting to the satanic program to bring the goodness of God into disrepute and cause thousands of sinners to stumble over such Christian examples and to reject a God that would will this kind of life upon His children...If all Christians would have faith in God and carry out the simple laws of prosperity laid down in these passages . . . God would bless them in abundance so that they could have more and more to help others with. The all-inclusive law of prosperity is to consecrate oneself to help others and to use what we have and God will give the increase." [14]

So, how are we to think? We should think like God thinks. We should believe His Word. We should get wealth. We should give generously! Let's think like these scriptures . . .

Luke 12:32 (NKJV)

Do not fear, little flock, for it is your Father's good pleasure to give you the kingdom.

What does the Father desire to give you? _____

How would you define "good pleasure"? _____

Matthew 7:11

So if you sinful people know how to give good gifts to your children, how much more will your heavenly Father give good gifts to those who ask him.

Is the Father a giver or a taker? _____

What does He give to those who ask? _____

Matthew 5:16

Let your light so shine before men, that they may see your good works and glorify your Father in heaven.

Having a generous spirit, among other things, is one way to let our light shine.

How does giving shine a light before men? _____

What will our good works cause others to do? _____

Proverbs 3:9-10

Honor the LORD with your wealth and with the best part of everything you produce.[10] Then he will fill your barns with grain, and your vats will overflow with good wine.

What are we to do with our wealth? _____

_____

What will the Lord do for us? _____

_____

Luke 6:38

Give, and you will receive. Your gift will return to you in full—pressed down, shaken together to make room for more, running over, and poured into your lap. The amount you give will determine the amount you get back.

If we give, what will happen? _____

How will our gifts return to us? _____

_____

In what measure or amount will we receive?_____

_____

When it comes to giving, God always finds a way to cause us to receive back what we give away. Not only that, it comes back to us in the amount we gave—in a multiplied measure and running over!

Isaiah 32:8

But a generous man devises generous things, and by generosity he shall stand.

What do generous people devise? _____

What will his generosity cause him to do? _____

_____

My sister Rhonda and her husband Tim are missionaries to Mexico City and several years ago while boarding a flight, Rhonda depicted this passage beautifully. She was seated comfortably in a first class seat when she noticed an American soldier in uniform boarding the plane. Immediately, the Lord prompted her to devise a generous thing! She decided to give the solider her first class seat and take his coach seat. Once she received permission from the flight attendant, she made the switch with the soldier, much to his joyful surprise and to the applause of the rest of the passengers! Later, the flight attendant told my sister how much her act of generosity had touched her and everyone on the plane. Meanwhile, back in coach, the attendants brought my sister a first class meal and treated her like a VIP! Isn't that such a great story? I love everything about this spirit of generosity!

So far, we've looked at 12 Proofs God Wants His People to Get Wealth, 12 Reasons Some People Will Never Get Wealth, as well as Our Mindset When It Comes to Wealth and Generosity. At this point, you may have a few questions. Let's address some of the most common questions.

COMMON QUESTIONS ABOUT WEALTH AND GENEROSITY

1. Isn't money the root of all evil?

1 Timothy 6:8-11,17-19

So if we have enough food and clothing, let us be content. [9] But people who long to be rich fall into temptation and are trapped by many foolish and harmful desires that plunge them into ruin and destruction. [10] For the love of money is the root of all kinds of evil. And some people, craving money, have wandered from the true faith and pierced themselves with many sorrows.[11] But you, Timothy, are a man of God; so run from all these evil things. Pursue righteousness and a godly life, along with faith, love, perseverance, and gentleness . . . [17] Teach those who are rich in this world not to be proud and not to trust in their money, which is so unreliable. Their trust should be in God, who richly gives us all we need for our enjoyment. [18] Tell them to use their money to do good. They should be rich in good works and generous to those in need, always being ready to share with others. [19] By doing this they will be storing up their treasure as a good foundation for the future so that they may experience true life.

Money itself is not evil. It's the love of money that is evil. Money is neutral. It's neither evil nor good. It's what we do with money that makes it evil or good. Money is simply a tool for doing good or evil.

You can see this dichotomy by comparing verse 9 and 10 with verses 17 and 18. When people love money, they crave and pursue it and end up wandering from true faith and experiencing sorrow. When people love God, they crave and pursue Him and use their money as a tool to enjoy life and to give generously to those in need.

In verse 17, we see the main point of these passages. The key point is trust! Money is not the issue. What our hearts love and trust is the issue. So, let's trust God and not money. Let's love God and not money.

2. Isn't wealth a sign of being worldly?

1 John 2:16

For the world offers only a craving for physical pleasure, a craving for everything we see, and pride in our achievements and possessions. These are not from the Father, but are from this world.

It's true that those who are wealthy face certain worldly temptations to fulfill the lusts of the flesh (physical pleasures), the lusts of the eyes (craving everything we see), and the pride of life in acquiring and boasting (in our achievements and possessions). But it's not just the wealthy who face these temptations; a poor person can be tempted with these worldly things, just as much as those who are wealthy. In some cases, a poor person may be even more tempted to lust after something he is unable to obtain. I know I have been in seasons where I didn't have enough money coming in, and I spent way too much time thinking about money. That's my nice way of saying that I was worrying about how I was going to make my Ramen noodles last a little longer while being jealous of my wealthy, generous neighbors. They were praising God, grilling steaks, and eating shrimp-on-the-barbie; I was poor, worrying, and envious. In that case, who was the worldly one?

Worldliness is a matter of the heart, not the pocketbook. Having wealth is not about houses, cars, or material things; it's about options. Wealth gives you options. When you are free financially, you can make choices from the heart, not from the pocketbook.

3. **Doesn't the Bible say it is impossible for a rich man to enter into the kingdom of God?**

Mark 10:17-27 (NKJV)

Now as He was going out on the road, one came running, knelt before Him, and asked Him, "Good Teacher, what shall I do that I may inherit eternal life?" [18] So Jesus said to him, "Why do you call Me good? No one is good but One, *that is,* God. [19] You know the commandments: 'Do not commit adultery,' 'Do not murder,' 'Do not steal,' 'Do not bear false witness,' 'Do not defraud,' 'Honor your father and your mother.'" [20] And he answered and said to Him, "Teacher, all these things I have kept from my youth." [21] Then Jesus, looking at him, loved him, and said to him, "One thing you lack: Go your way, sell whatever you have and give to the poor, and you will have treasure in heaven; and come, take up the cross, and follow Me." [22] But he was sad at this word, and went away sorrowful, for he had great possessions. [23] Then Jesus looked around and said to His disciples, "How hard it is for those who have riches to enter the kingdom of God!" [24] And the disciples were astonished at His words. But Jesus answered again and said to them, "Children, how hard it is for those who trust in riches to enter the kingdom of God! [25] It is easier for a camel to go through the eye of a needle than for a rich man to enter the kingdom of God." [26] And they were greatly astonished, saying among themselves, "Who then can be saved?" [27] But Jesus looked at them and said, "With men *it is* impossible, but not with God; for with God all things are possible."

This passage has tripped up believers for centuries. Was Jesus saying that rich people can't be saved? Was He telling us to avoid being rich? Again, when it comes to money, we will see that the issue is trust. Let's look in detail at this passage.

This is the story of the rich young ruler. Jesus loved this man. After a series of questions and answers, Jesus asked him to sell all he had and give it to the poor, then come and follow Him. (Notice: Jesus didn't tell him to give all that he had to the poor. He said to *sell* all that he had and give the proceeds to the poor.) The rich young ruler went away sad, for he had a great number of possessions but wouldn't part with them. The truth is, his possessions had him, and he loved and trusted in his riches and possessions more than he loved Jesus.

Jesus made it clear that it is hard (not impossible but hard) for those who trust in their riches to enter the kingdom of God, not because God is unmerciful or unwilling for them to trust Him but because the wealthy grow accustomed to trusting in their own wealth for prestige, influence, status, and purchasing power. This position in life can be very gratifying to the flesh, so it's often difficult for those who are rich to stop trusting in their riches and trust in God. Jesus is just stating a fact of human nature. It isn't impossible for a rich person to stop trusting in his own wealth and to follow Jesus, but it's more difficult for him than it would be for a person who has nothing to lose. This makes logical sense, because it's the nature of the carnal, five-physical-senses-ruled man.

Jesus told us how difficult this choice is when he talked about the difficulty of a camel going through the eye of a needle. Some Bible scholars believe Jesus was referring to a geographic area called "the eye of a needle," which camels had difficulty passing through. Others scholars believe Jesus was literally speaking of a needle and thread and the impossible task of putting a camel through the eye of a needle.

Either way, we get the idea that man's way of obtaining salvation through trusting in his money, influence, and power is impossible, but God's way of obtaining salvation through faith by grace is possible. In other words, the rich and the poor alike must approach God the same way—by trusting in Him. When we do things God's way, nothing is impossible!

Again, the point of this passage, among others, is not that it's wrong to be rich but that it's wrong to trust in riches. Let's look at a few additional scriptures.

Psalm 49:6-7

They trust in their wealth and boast of great riches. ⁷ Yet they cannot redeem themselves from death by paying a ransom to God.

Psalm 52:7

Look what happens to mighty warriors who do not trust in God. They trust their wealth instead and grow more and more bold in their wickedness.

Proverbs 3:5-6

Trust in the Lord with all your heart; do not depend on your own understanding. ⁶ Seek his will in all you do, and he will show you which path to take.

When we trust in our riches rather than in God and His Word, we can be deceived and sidetracked by the deceitful lure of money. That's exactly what Jesus said, "And the cares of this world, the deceitfulness of riches, and the desires for other things entering in choke the word, and it becomes unfruitful" (Mark 4:19, NKJV). The deceitfulness of riches chokes the word in our lives, and we become unfruitful.

As you can see, God is not against us having nice things, but He doesn't want the nice things to have us! After all, God gives us all things richly so that we may enjoy them. The thing that displeases God is when we trust and love our riches more than or rather than Him. So, let's trust the Lord with all our heart and use wealth appropriately!

4. Isn't God's primary concern our spiritual lives, not our financial or material lives?

Yes, His main concern is our spiritual health and our relationship with Him, but that doesn't mean our physical, material, and financial needs are not of interest to Him. In light of all of the scriptures we've look at so far, we can see that the Lord cares about our spirit, soul, and body. God is interested in our material, financial, and physical needs. We see this in Matthew 6 and 3 John 2.

Matthew 6:25-33 (NKJV)

Therefore I say to you, do not worry about your life, what you will eat or what you will drink; nor about your body, what you will put on. Is not life more than food and the body more than clothing? [26] Look at the birds of the air, for they neither sow nor reap nor gather into barns; yet your heavenly Father feeds them. Are you not of more value than they? [27] Which of you by worrying can add one cubit to his stature? [28] So why do you worry about clothing? Consider the lilies of the field, how they grow: they neither toil nor spin; [29] and yet I say to you that even Solomon in all his glory was not arrayed like one of these. [30] Now if God so clothes the grass of the field, which today is, and tomorrow is thrown into the oven, *will* He not much more *clothe* you, O you of little faith? [31] Therefore do not worry, saying, "What shall we eat?" or "What shall we drink?" or "What shall we wear?" [32] For after all these things the Gentiles seek. For your heavenly Father knows that you need all these things. [33] But seek first the kingdom of God and His righteousness, and all these things shall be added to you.

3 John 2 (NKJV)

Beloved, I pray that you may prosper in all things and be in health, just as your soul prospers.

Interestingly, Jesus talked more about money, material things, abundance, prosperity, faithfulness, and stewardship than He did about being born again and going to heaven. If Jesus emphasized these things, we should be very comfortable in learning about them. As Christians, we should not apologize for, ignore, or dismiss discussions related to money, wealth, prosperity, or financial success.

5. Isn't stewardship more important than getting wealth?

Stewardship, as well as budgeting and learning contentment, is a huge indicator of Christian maturity. The Bible has a lot to say about stewardship and the ultimate reckoning of our accounts. God is very interested in our role as good stewards of everything He's given us: our time, gifts, talents, relationships, health, and our spiritual and financial resources, as we shall see in Matthew 25. He wants us to invest, maximize, and increase what we have been given. Let's look at this passage.

Matthew 25:14-29

Again, the Kingdom of Heaven can be illustrated by the story of a man going on a long trip. He called together his servants and entrusted his money to them while he was gone. [15] He gave five bags of silver to one, two bags of silver to another, and one bag of silver to the last—dividing it in proportion to their abilities. He then left on his trip. [16] The servant who received the five bags of silver began to invest the money and earned five more. [17] The servant with two bags of silver also went to work and earned two more. [18] But the servant who received the one bag of silver dug a hole in the ground and hid the master's money. [19] After a long time their master returned from his trip and called them to give an account of how they had used his money. [20] The servant to whom he had entrusted the five bags of silver came forward with five more and said, "Master, you gave me five bags of silver to invest, and I have earned five more." [21] The master was full of praise. "Well done, my good and faithful servant. You have been faithful in handling this small amount, so now I will give you many more responsibilities. Let's celebrate together!" [22] The servant who had received the two bags of silver came forward and said, "Master, you gave me two bags of silver to invest, and I have earned two more." [23] The master said, "Well done, my good and faithful servant. You have been faithful in handling this small amount, so now I will give you many more responsibilities. Let's celebrate together!" [24] Then the servant with the one bag of silver came and said, "Master, I knew you were a harsh man, harvesting crops you didn't plant and gathering crops you didn't cultivate. [25] I was afraid I would lose your money, so I hid it in the earth. Look, here is your money back." [26] But the master replied, "You wicked and lazy servant! If you knew I harvested crops I didn't plant and gathered crops I didn't cultivate, [27] why didn't you deposit my money in the bank? At least I could have gotten some interest on it." [28] Then he ordered, "Take the money from this servant, and give it to the one with the ten bags of silver. [29] To those who use well what they are given, even more will be given, and they will have an abundance. But from those who do nothing, even what little they have will be taken away."

Can you see that stewardship, getting wealth, and generosity all go together?

LET'S GET PRACTICAL

Ok friends, we've covered a lot of ground in this first chapter. Are you hanging in there? For some of you, your heart is jumping up and down with hope-filled joy and you can't wait to continue in our study! Others of you may be reading many of these scriptures for the first time, and your head is on the verge of tilt. That's perfectly normal. Let's wrap up this session with two practical to dos:

1) Make a quality decision to take your time and read all the scriptures we've cover in this book. It takes time reading and rereading God's Word on this subject to renew your mind and allow God to give you the revelation you need to build your faith on His desire for your wealth and generosity.

2) Pray and ask God for His help.

"Dear Father, I am so thankful for Your Word. It is the truth. I am beginning to get a better working knowledge of Your plan to help me get wealth and give generously. I ask You to continue to fill me with the knowledge of Your will in all wisdom and spiritual understanding. Help me to renew my mind to see, believe, and experience wealth and generosity the way You desire. Thank You for innovative ideas and for leading me by Your Word and by Your Spirit into a successful and generous life. In Jesus' name. Amen."

JOURNAL ENTRY

To get the most out of this chapter, take a few moments to journal your thoughts and/or prayers.

_____

_____

_____

_____

_____

_____

_____

_____

_____

_____

_____

_____

_____

_____

SESSION 2
THE BLESSING OF THE TITHE

———◆———

The story is told of two men who were marooned on an island. One man paced back and forth, worried and scared. The other man sat back and enjoyed sunning himself. The first man said to the second man, "Aren't you afraid we are about to die?"

"No," said the second man. "I make $100,000 per week, and I tithe faithfully to my church every week. My pastor will find me."

If that were a true story, his pastor would definitely find him!

Unfortunately in some circles, when you mention tithing, sparks start to fly, fangs come out (of nice looking Christians), and the discussion can almost get as heated as a conversation about the rapture of the Church. Are you pre-tithe, mid-tithe, or post-tithe?

So, when it comes to tithing, let's identify some of the legitimate questions people ask:

- What is tithing?
- Isn't tithing just an Old Testament principle?

- Is tithing a command for New Testament Christians?

- Are we under the law or under grace when it comes to tithing?

- Shouldn't we be led by the Spirit in our giving, rather than tithing?

- From which amount of income is a person supposed to tithe, the net or the gross?

- Can I tithe four percent of my income rather than ten percent?

- Where should I give my tithe: to my church, to support a missionary, to help a friend or relative in need, or to feed hungry children?

- What's the difference between tithes, offerings, and alms?

As we go through this session, we'll do our best to answer these questions and more.

Christian leaders seem to have mixed views on tithing. Although a large number of leaders believe the Bible teaches that Christians ought to tithe, others believe Christians don't have to tithe but should be led by the Spirit in giving generously. Still others suggest that any New Testament believer who regularly gives *below* ten percent of his income to his church is probably not being led by the Spirit.

So, dear reader, I might as well let the cat out of the bag. If asked my view on tithing, I would select "all of the above!" I believe the Bible teaches that Christians ought to tithe, and I believe that believers should be led by the Spirit in their giving. I also believe that any New Testament believer who regularly gives below ten percent of his or her income to build Christ's church is probably not being led by the Spirit. (Check. Check. Is this mic still on? If I lost you there, let me just say, "It was nice to have met you! Have a great life. Best wishes! Don't be

mad. Still love you. Please don't write a mean Amazon review. Peace."
#dropthemic)

But here's the thing. Doing all of these things—tithing, being led by the Spirit, not giving less than ten percent of our income to the Lord—should be the normal response of a Christian who's experienced the extravagant love and generous mercy of the Lord. We should not view giving as a duty, payment, or law abiding work because then we slip right into a self-righteous, legalistic relationship with God. We need to understand that our response to God in every area, including tithing, is not an if-then but a because-then proposition! In other words, in the if-then mindset, we think, "If I tithe, then God will bless me." As if when I push the right buttons and pull the right levers, God is obligated to bless me. No! God has already blessed us in Christ with all kinds of things—forgiveness, righteousness, favor, acceptance, approval, freedom, peace, healing, and success—so because of His amazing love and generosity, I am free and compelled to give Him one hundred percent of everything I have and everything I am. So then, giving ten percent of my income to His priority, the church, is the least I can do!

Can you see that paradigm shift on this topic? This is a major basic, so if you need to reread it, go right ahead!

Now, let me add an addendum. It may take a bit of time to get there. It took me a few years of being a Christian to finally catch onto the idea of giving. I was a taker for the first few years of my Christian life, but as I grew in the Lord, being a giver became my desired lifestyle and it started with tithing. That's why we are starting with this topic of tithing.

What's important is not what I believe, but what do you believe? The best thing to do is dig into the Scriptures to hear from God and decide for yourself what you believe about tithing. In this session, since this is a basics book, we are going to keep our study simple while hopefully encouraging, challenging, and giving you enough tools to make your own decisions. Bottom line, whatever you learn about wealth and generosity or about tithing can't just be great theory; it has to work.

You have to wonder if God is so good and interested in blessing our lives, why then are so many Christians poor and broke? Why does it seem like many of God's people—hard working people—live with a paycheck-to-paycheck mentality or worse, in poverty? Why do some people seem to be able to climb out of poverty, get out of debt, and enter into the generous lifestyle, while others remain stuck in lack and always coming up short? God is not blessing one of His children while overlooking another, is He?

If God is a loving Father to all of His children, He cannot be pleased when we struggle to make it, nor can He be pleased when He's given us an entrance ramp to financial victory and we refuse to access it. I wonder if we've missed something in the way we've viewed tithing and giving in general. Maybe we've looked at tithing as a take when really it's a give. Maybe we've viewed it as a work we had to do to get blessed, rather than as a response we get to do because God has blessed us.

Perhaps we thought God was trying to take something from us, when really He was trying to give something to us. After all, do we really think God needs our money? This God whose streets are paved with gold, does He need our money? Perhaps through the tithe, God has put into play an equitable way for everyone to exercise their faith and rise above the world economy and into the flow of His blessed economy. Maybe it's the *blessing* of the tithe, not the *bummer* of the tithe.

Let's see what the Bible says about the what, why, who, when, where, and how of tithing.

WHAT IS TITHING?

What is the tithe or tithing?

By definition, the tithe is ten percent or one-tenth of our increase or income. The tithe or tithing represents the giving of one-tenth of a person's earnings. The Hebrew word for "tithe" is *ma'aser*. It literally means the tenth part or the payment of a tenth part.

Leviticus 27:30 (NKJV)

And all the tithe of the land, *whether* of the seed of the land *or* of the fruit of the tree, *is* the LORD's: it *is* holy unto the LORD.

Who does the tithe belong to? _____

What is the tithe called? _____

What percent of our produce, increase, or income is considered to be the tithe? _____

As you can see, the tithe represents ten percent of our income and is called "holy," set apart as the Lord's. When we give the Lord His ten percent, it sets apart (or redeems) our remaining ninety percent to be blessed.

Deuteronomy 14:23 (TLB)

The purpose of tithing is to teach you always to put God first in your lives.

What's the purpose of tithing? _____

Tithing is an act of worship, devotion, trust, and faith.

Malachi 3:10 (NCV)

"Bring to the storehouse a full tenth of what you earn . . . Test me in this," says the LORD All-Powerful. "I will open the windows of heaven for you and pour out all the blessings you need."

What are we to bring to God? _____

Where are we to bring our tithe? _____

What did God challenge us to do? _____

What did God promise He would do? _____

1 Corinthians 16:2 (TLB)

On every Lord's Day each of you should put aside something from what you have earned during the week, and use it for this offering. The amount depends on how much the Lord has helped you earn.

When are you supposed to bring the percentage you've put aside to the Lord? _____

The Apostle Paul is clearly telling the New Testament believers they should be in the habit of setting aside a portion of their earnings each week to give to the Lord. (In this case, Paul was referring to a special offering for the poor saints in Jerusalem.) Based upon Paul's own upbringing and from the rest of the scriptures, we have every reason to believe Paul was a tither. You get the idea here that he advocated proportional giving as a regular practice for believers.

WHY SHOULD WE TITHE?

Here are two good reasons to tithe:

1) Tithing honors the Lord.

2) Tithing provides food (spiritual and natural) in God's house.

The tithe honors and belongs to the Lord. In the same way that worship, gratitude, and praise belong to the Lord, so too, does the tithe. (And, we don't see anywhere in Scripture where the Lord rescinded His tithe.)

As mentioned, tithing is not an obligation, requirement, or duty to perform. Tithing is a blessing to enter into! When you begin to look at tithing as an opportunity, as an entrance ramp for trusting the Lord and entering into His thriving economy, it will change your entire perspective and motivation.

As we continue in our study of God's Word, I believe you will see that giving God at least ten percent of our income (the tithe) from a heart of love, faith, trust and gratitude—not from duty or obligation—is the starting point for Christians who want to step into the blessed flow of God's economy. Keep in mind that while the tithe is technically ten percent, it's not the ten percent that activates God's blessing. It's our *faith,* not our works, that put the blessings of God's economy into motion. Let me say that one more time because it's easy to miss it. We tithe by faith because we love God more than money, and the Lord rewards our faith. We don't tithe as a work, as if we are pushing a button, pulling a lever, or jumping through a hoop in order to get God to bless us.

Leviticus 27:30

One-tenth of the produce of the land, whether grain from the fields or fruit from the trees, belongs to the LORD and must be set apart to him as holy.

What belongs to the Lord? _____

Proverbs 3:9-10

Trust in the LORD with all your heart; do not depend on your own understanding. [6] Seek his will in all you do, and he will show you which path to take. [7] Don't be impressed with your own wisdom. Instead, fear the LORD and turn away from evil. [8] Then you will have healing for your body and strength for your bones. [9] Honor the LORD with your wealth and with the best part of everything you produce. [10] Then he will fill your barns with grain, and your vats will overflow with good wine.

What are we to do with our whole heart? _____

What are we to seek? _____

What are we to not be impressed with? _____

What is the result of putting our trust (faith) in the Lord? _____

_____

What are we to do with our wealth and the "best part" (or first ten percent) of everything we produce? _____

What happens when we honor the Lord with our wealth? _____

_____

Malachi 3:10

"Bring all the tithes into the storehouse so there will be enough food in my Temple. If you do," says the LORD of Heaven's Armies, "I will open the windows of heaven for you. I will pour out a blessing so great you won't have enough room to take it in! Try it! Put me to the test!"

What allows there to be enough food in God's temple?

_____

There can't be "food" (some versions say "meat") in God's house, the local church, unless tithes are brought to the storehouse of the local church.

We see a twofold application to the words, "food in My house."

First, many times in Scripture, we see "food" or "meat" as a reference to the mature things of God's Word, or "revelation knowledge." Did you know you can expect God to give you "meat"—revelation knowledge and understanding of the mature things of God's Word?

Second, it takes finances to give a church "meat," the provisions it needs to pioneer, build, grow, hire staff, train church members, and expand a church and its outreach efforts locally and around the world. The tithe was and is God's plan for financing His Church and the outreach of His Gospel around the world.

WHO SHOULD TITHE?

If you're wondering who should tithe, I'd say only those to whom God has given one hundred percent of everything! Since that includes all of us, let's take a closer look.

You may wonder, "What about the rich people, many of them Christians, who work hard, make lots of money, and don't tithe?" Well, living in God's economy is about more than being rich. The blessings that follow the faith of a tither include much more than a fat paycheck. Often, we don't realize the blessings of a well-greased life that include wisdom, ideas, favor, healthy relationships, good health, or having a car, tires, appliances, a house, and other possessions that don't seem to wear out quite as quickly as others. There is a host of other seemingly intangible blessings God gives to people of faith. He truly does open the windows of heaven and pour out blessings. He truly does rebuke the enemy from devouring things in our lives. Not to mention, Jesus said that our generous life stores up treasures in heaven where moth and rust cannot destroy. You can take this to the bank (literally). Without a tithing and a generous spirit, all the hard work and money in the world are just that: hard work and money. However, when you combine work and wealth with faith and the practice of tithing, you enter into God's economy.

You may also wonder, "What about people who are regular tithers, but their lives do not appear to be blessed?" Well, to have a holistic view, there are a couple of things we should consider.

Tithing isn't the magic bullet or lever for pulling down a healthy, wealthy, and trouble free life. Jesus said that everyone would face trials and tribulations in this world, but I would present to you (and the jury) an observation that people of faith who honor the Lord with their lives and income often seem to have more resources for overcoming those adversities.

Some folks may be disciplined tithers, but if they have a poor work ethic and/or a lack of discipline in their spending, they can end up being poor. Tithing isn't Tinkerbelle dust we sprinkle into an offering plate with the hopes that God won't notice that we are being slackers on the job or undisciplined in our stewardship. Tithing works in concert with things like faith, wisdom, integrity, faithfulness, and being diligent in our work and stewardship; for without those things, there's no wealth from which to tithe.

Who should tithe? Those who love the Lord, right? If we say that we love the Lord and He's first in our lives, the quickest way to verify such a claim is to look at our bank account. The legendary Rev. Billy Graham once said, "Give me five minutes with a person's checkbook, and I will tell you where their heart is . . . A checkbook is a theological document. It will tell you who and what you worship." (Just in case you don't know, checks are like a debit card made from paper and some people still use them—like my husband. These days, more and more people use digital and online giving as their primary way to engage in regular tithing.)

Matthew 6:21

Wherever your treasure is, there the desires of your heart will also be.

Jesus said the desires of our heart could be identified by what?

WHEN IS THE TITHE IN EFFECT?

Here's the big question: Is there an expiration date on tithing? (Or, does the tithe still belong to God?) Let's look at tithing past and present by studying three historical time frames for the tithe; tithing before the law, tithing under the law, and tithing after the law.

We know God commanded Moses and His people to tithe under the law. But what about before the law and what about after the law?

The law, commonly known as the Mosaic Law, was given to Moses and made up of three parts: the moral law (the Ten Commandments), the ceremonial law (the rules for worship), and the civil law (the way people should govern themselves). The Mosaic Law came into existence 430 years after God had made promises and established His covenant with Abraham (Genesis 12:1-3, Galatians 3:17), and the law ended when Jesus shed His blood on the cross.

So, let's start with tithing before the law.

TITHING BEFORE THE LAW

The first reference to tithing in Scripture is found in Genesis.

Genesis 14:18-20

And Melchizedek, the king of Salem and a priest of God Most High, brought Abram some bread and wine. Melchizedek blessed Abram with this blessing: "Blessed be Abram by God Most High, Creator of heaven and earth. And blessed be God Most High, who has defeated your enemies for you." Then Abram gave Melchizedek a tenth of all the goods he had recovered.

What did Abram give to Melchizedek? _____

We don't know what "all the goods" included, but we do know it was his increase, income, and valuable spoils of battle.

Abraham was not under the law that required him to tithe, but we see that he chose to tithe as an act of love, faith, and respect for the king of Salem. (Abraham understood the "because/then" principle we talked about earlier!) In this instance, Abram (Abraham) tithed years before the law was ever instituted. Abram tithed out of a heart that was willing to give, not under compulsion or the law.

Notice the types and shadows in this passage. Abram is called the father of our faith (Romans 4:11-12), and Melchizedek is a king, a type of Jesus, the King of kings (Hebrews 7:15-17). Through their interactions, words, and behaviors, we see a preview of what our faith-based relationship with Jesus would be like. Melchizedek brought Abram bread and wine, a clear reference to Jesus coming to earth to lay down His life and shed His blood for us. Melchizedek was a king of Salem (modern Jerusalem) and a priest of God Most High, another clear reference to Jesus, King of kings and our High Priest who will one day rule and reign from His throne in Jerusalem. Melchizedek pronounced a blessing to God and the blessing of God over Abram, another clear reference to all of the blessings we've been given in Christ. Then, notice what Abram did (not because it was the law or a rule or required) from the faith and love in his heart. His heart of appreciation prompted him to give Melchizedek ten percent of all the goods he had recovered—the tithe. In this case, tithing was clearly *not* an act of the law but an act of faith and love.

Genesis 28:20-22

Then Jacob made this vow: "If God will indeed be with me and protect me on this journey, and if he will provide me with food and clothing, and if I return safely to my father's home, then the LORD will certainly be my God. And this memorial pillar I have set up will become a place for worshiping God, and I will present to God a tenth of everything he gives me."

What did Jacob vow to give to the Lord? _____

Jacob was not obligated to give the Lord a tenth according to the law, because the law didn't exist at that time. Jacob gave his tithe to the Lord out of a heart of gratitude, not compulsion. Again, an act of love, not law.

I wonder where Jacob learned about tithing? Is it possible that his grandfather Abram had told Jacob's father, Isaac, tithing stories about God's blessings that Isaac passed on to Jacob? It's evident God's people were tithers before the law required it! They tithed ten percent of all they had because they loved God and they must have known something about God's generous will to bless them.

Spoiler Alert: An interesting side note is that Abram (Abraham) and Jacob were some of the wealthiest persons in the Bible! So wealthy in fact, their accumulation of goods, employees, herds, and lands became quite a management issue. Genesis 24:1 (NKJV) describes the end of Abraham's life, "Now Abraham was old, well advanced in age; and the LORD had blessed Abraham in all things." Tithing certainly didn't hurt Abraham!

TITHING UNDER THE LAW

The law of the tithe was instituted under the Mosaic Law. As mentioned, this law came into existence 430 years after God made promises and established His covenant with Abraham. During this time, under the law, God's people were expected to tithe by giving the Lord ten percent of their income and increase. Tithing was not optional. Under the law, God's people were expected to live by the if-then principle. If they tithed, then they could expect certain blessings, and if they didn't tithe, they could expect to be "cursed with a curse."

Under the law, here is what God expected . . .

Exodus 23:19

As you harvest your crops, bring the very best of the first harvest to the house of the Lord your God . . .

What did the Lord want the Israelites to bring to the house of the Lord? _____

The Lord wants the very best of the very first harvest brought to His house. Leviticus defines this even further.

Leviticus 27:30-32

One-tenth of the produce of the land, whether grain from the fields or fruit from the trees, belongs to the Lord and must be set apart to him as holy. If you want to buy back the Lord's tenth of the grain or fruit, you must pay its value, plus 20 percent. Count off every tenth animal from your herds and flocks and set them apart for the Lord as holy.

Again, what belongs to the Lord? _____

What is the tithe set apart as? _____

According to the commandment of the Lord, the Israelites were supposed to tithe one-tenth of the produce of the land to the Lord. It belonged to Him. That was the law. And there was a huge penalty for those who failed to tithe. Notice, if a person under the Law didn't give the Lord one-tenth of his or her increase, the Lord expected an additional twenty percent penalty be paid. In other words, under the law, if a person wanted to keep his tithes and not pay them to the Lord, he was required as a penalty to pay an additional twenty percent!

Cleary, the tithe belonged to the Lord. But, here's the big question: Is there any scripture reference in either the Old or New Testament that tells us that this has expired? If so, when did the tithe quit belonging to the Lord? If not, then is it safe to say the tithe still belongs to the Lord? (I rest my case, your Honor.)

Deuteronomy 14:22-26

You must set aside a tithe of your crops—one-tenth of all the crops you harvest each year. 23 Bring this tithe to the designated place of worship—the place the Lord your God chooses for his name to be honored—and eat it there in his presence. This applies to your tithes of grain, new wine, olive oil, and the firstborn males of your flocks and herds. Doing this will teach you always to fear the Lord your God. 24 Now when the Lord your God blesses you with a good harvest, the place of worship he chooses for his name to be honored might be too far for you to bring the tithe. 25 If so, you may sell the tithe portion of your crops and herds, put the money in a pouch, and go to the place the Lord your God has chosen. 26 When you arrive, you may use the money to buy any kind of food you want—cattle, sheep, goats, wine, or other alcoholic drink. Then feast there in the presence of the Lord your God and celebrate with your household.

What percentage of our harvest (increase, income, earnings) are we supposed to set aside for the tithe? _____

Where were God's people supposed to bring the tithe? _____

_____

God expected His people to tithe one-tenth of their increase and bring it to the place of worship. If the place of worship was too far away to attend on a regular basis, He expected them to sell the tithe portion of their crops and herds so they could bring the funds to the place of worship when they attended. You will note that these funds were to be used by the house of worship to provide food and drink for God's people to be fed as they celebrated the Lord's Presence. (We will talk more about this as we continue our study.)

What was bringing their tithe to their place of worship supposed to teach them? _____

Malachi 3:8-12

Should people cheat God? Yet you have cheated me! But you ask, "What do you mean? When did we ever cheat you?" "You have cheated me of the tithes and offerings due to me. ⁹ You are under a curse, for your whole nation has been cheating me. ¹⁰ Bring all the tithes into the storehouse so there will be enough food in my Temple. If you do," says the LORD of Heaven's Armies, "I will open the windows of heaven for you. I will pour out a blessing so great you won't have enough room to take it in! Try it! Put me to the test! ¹¹ Your crops will be abundant, for I will guard them from insects and disease. Your grapes will not fall from the vine before they are ripe," says the Lord of Heaven's Armies. ¹² "Then all nations will call you blessed, for your land will be such a delight," says the LORD of Heaven's Armies.

In what way can God be cheated? _____

As we have clearly seen, when Israel was under the law, they were required to tithe; if they did not, God considered it robbery! To rob or cheat someone presupposes that the item taken was his or hers to begin with. (Notice in verse 8, He said, "you cheated me of the tithes and offerings." We will discuss the subject of offerings in the next section, but for now, we will focus on the tithe.)

What happened to those who cheated God in tithes (and offerings)?

_____

What do you think it means to be "cursed with a curse"?

_____

A curse is bad enough, but to be cursed with a curse; that's a curse squared! Thank God we're not under the law these days! Nonetheless, we get the idea that being stingy, selfish, and covetous isn't a good idea, and that God's blessings are attached to being full of faith and generous.

What did the Lord want His people to do with all the tithes?

_____

Why did He want the tithe brought to the storehouse? _____

_____

What challenge did God give His people? _____

_____

What did God promise to those who brought their tithe to the storehouse? _____

What did God say people would call tithers? _____

_____

In this passage, we see the emphasis, longing, and boldness with which God tells His people to bring the tithes to His storehouses. I hear a God who wanted to give His people blessings, not a God who wanted to take people's money. I believe that's still God's heart today. He wants His people to take Him at His Word as they bring their tithe to the place of worship so they will be blessed with both spiritual and natural "meat" and so that He can open the windows of heaven and pour out blessings over their lives.

TITHING AFTER THE LAW

So, what about the requirement to tithe after the law, in the times in which we live—in these New Testament, New Covenant times? This is the time frame we are most interested in, right? Again we ask, has tithing expired? John the Baptist came preaching about Jesus, the Lamb of God, who would take away the sins of the world—and fulfill the law! After Jesus fulfilled the law, Christ's followers would not be under the *Old Testament law*, but would be called to live under the *New Testament Law of Christ* also known as the royal law of love. Let's see how this affects our decision to tithe.

Luke 16:16

Until John the Baptist, the law of Moses and the messages of the prophets were your guides. But now the Good News of the Kingdom of God is preached, and everyone is eager to get in.

When did John say the principles governing the obligation to obey the law and the Old Testament prophets ended?

When did the principles governing obedience to the kingdom of God begin? _____

1 Corinthians 9:20-21

When I was with the Jews, I lived like a Jew to bring the Jews to Christ. When I was with those who follow the Jewish law, I too lived under that law. Even though I am not subject to the law, I did this so I could bring to Christ those who are under the law. [21] When I am with the Gentiles who do not follow the Jewish law, I too live apart from that law so I can bring them to Christ. But I do not ignore the law of God; I obey the law of Christ.

In this passage, the apostle Paul is talking about how believers are to relate to unbelievers in order to lead them to Christ. He makes an interesting point in verse 21.

I do not ignore the _____;
I obey the _____.

As believers we are not under the law any longer, but we are under *the Law of Christ*. Many scholars believe the Law of Christ is described by Jesus as the new commandment, "A new commandment I give to you, that you love one another; as I have loved you, that you also love one another" (John 13:34, KJV). James calls the Law of Christ the royal law: "Yes indeed, it is good when you obey the royal law as found in the Scriptures: "Love your neighbor as yourself" (James 2:8). In other words, as Christians, everything we do is supposed to be motivated by love (the Law of Christ) and not by the law. It starts with the fact that Jesus loves us! We love Him because He first loved us. The result of His love is that we love God and we love one another. This is the because-then principle we've been talking about and the basis for everything we do, including our giving. We tithe because we love God and we love people, not because we are under the law. Do you see that?

Let's see what Jesus said about tithing.

Luke 11:42

What sorrow awaits you Pharisees! For you are careful to tithe even the tiniest income from your herb gardens, but you ignore justice and the love of God. You should tithe, yes, but do not neglect the more important things.

What did Jesus say about the ways the Pharisees were tithing?

_____

Did Jesus say they should stop tithing because He was going to institute the New Covenant? _____

What did Jesus say they should not neglect? _____

_____

Keep in mind when Jesus had this tithing conversation with the Pharisees, the religious leaders of His day, they were devout tithers down to the herb! In this exchange, Jesus had the perfect opportunity to tell these religious leaders that tithing was about to pass away because He was going to the cross to fulfill the law. However, Jesus didn't say, "Hey, good news everyone. I am here to fulfill the law. I'll go to the cross soon, and you'll no longer be under the law. Tithing is about to expire! Rejoice and go buy a new fishing boat!" Instead of letting them off the tithing hook, Jesus said, "You should tithe, yes, but do not neglect the more important things." He told them to tithe, but He rebuked them for missing the weightier matter of living out of a heart of love.

97

Hebrews 7:1-8 (NKJV)

For this Melchizedek, king of Salem, priest of the Most High God, who met Abraham returning from the slaughter of the kings and blessed him, [2] to whom also Abraham gave a tenth part of all, first being translated "king of righteousness," and then also king of Salem, meaning "king of peace," [3] without father, without mother, without genealogy, having neither beginning of days nor end of life, but made like the Son of God, remains a priest continually. [4] Now consider how great this man was, to whom even the patriarch Abraham gave a tenth of the spoils. [5] And indeed those who are of the sons of Levi, who receive the priesthood, have a commandment to receive tithes from the people according to the law, that is, from their brethren, though they have come from the loins of Abraham; [6] but he whose genealogy is not derived from them received tithes from Abraham and blessed him who had the promises. [7] Now beyond all contradiction the lesser is blessed by the better. [8] Here mortal men receive tithes, but there he receives them, of whom it is witnessed that he lives.

Remember this story? This passage refers to the account of Abraham (Abram) giving tithes to King Melchizedek before the law. It is also a reference to and a type of Christian believers giving tithes after the law to our King, Jesus Christ.

As Abraham gave tithes before the law to the high priest, Melchizedek, we (the seed of Abraham) give tithes after the law to our High Priest, Jesus Christ. Both Abraham and New Testament believers give tithes as an act of worship and love for God—not under compulsion as a duty of the law!

According to verse 8, when we give our tithes, who receives them here on earth? _____

According to verse 8, when we give our tithes, who receives them in heaven? _____

In other words, in the natural realm when we bring our tithes to our local church, it is mortal men and women on earth (that is ushers, secretaries, offering committees, and so on) who receive them for the Church. In the spiritual realm, in heaven, it is Jesus Christ himself who receives our tithes. It's helpful to keep this picture in mind as we bring our tithes to our local church each week. Whether we give our tithes through cash, a check, a digital wallet, texting, or online options, when we give to our church on earth, in heaven Jesus Christ is receiving our tithes as an act of our faith, love, and worship.

Note: Often people ask if they should tithe off their gross income or the net. Each person has to decide as a matter of personal conscience. There are people who tithe by faith off their gross, while others tithe by faith off their net. Whatever you choose to do, do it by faith. And then there's this. When you have a generous spirit, love God, and are passionate about His cause, you are going to give way more than ten percent of your income anyway. It's just who you are as a Christian. Giving your tithe to your local church, offerings to gospel ministries, and alms to initiatives that help people is just in your DNA. You have no interest in arguing about the "jot and tittle." (Had to throw some *King James* your way!) The truth is, giving God ten percent is entry-level Christianity. #truthbombjustexploded

Can you see that the blessing of tithing is for those before the law, under the law and after the law?

WHERE SHOULD WE BRING OUR TITHES?

Let's chat about a sacred cow. What if I want to give my tithe to the place of my choosing? Can I split up my tithe and give some here and some there?

From the whole of Scripture, it seems that the tithe has always been purposed to help support, build, and maintain God's house—known as the temple and storehouse of the Old Testament and the local church of the New Testament. Based on that precedent, it seems the tithe should be brought to your local church and not be divided up or given to anything other than your local church. This implies that you are planted in a God-ordained local church. I hope you are. Remember, 1 Corinthians 12:18? We are all a part of the body of Christ, His Church, and God sets us in His church body just where He wants us. What church has He set you in? Let me hit repeat. If you aren't committed to regularly attending a local church, I hope you will spend some time with God and in studying His Word to settle this matter. It is God's plan to build strong local churches and these days, it's in your best interest to be part of what God is doing on the earth in and through His local church! There's a reason Hebrews 10:25 was given to us: "And let us not neglect our meeting together, as some people do, but encourage one another, especially now that the day of his return is drawing near."

In some places, it has become the norm for Christian people to either not tithe at all or to give their tithe to a charitable work, other than the local church. While there are many worthy causes that should be supported (we'll talk about that in our next chapter), it seems apparent from Scripture that God's priority is for the tithe to go to His House. Let's look at this Biblical pattern.

Deuteronomy 12:11; 14:23

You must bring everything I command you—your burnt offerings, your sacrifices, your tithes, your sacred offerings, and your offerings to fulfill a vow—to the designated place of worship, the place the LORD your God chooses for his name to be honored . . . ²³ Bring this tithe to the designated place of worship—the place the LORD your God chooses for his name to be honored—and eat it there in his presence. This applies to your tithes of grain, new wine, olive oil, and the firstborn males of your flocks and herds. Doing this will teach you always to fear the LORD your God.

Where were the Israelites to bring their tithe? _____

_____

Haggai 1:2-11

"This is what the LORD of Heaven's Armies says: The people are saying, 'The time has not yet come to rebuild the house of the LORD.'"³ Then the LORD sent this message through the prophet Haggai: ⁴ "Why are you living in luxurious houses while my house lies in ruins? ⁵ This is what the LORD of Heaven's Armies says: Look at what's happening to you! ⁶ You have planted much but harvest little. You eat but are not satisfied. You drink but are still thirsty. You put on clothes but cannot keep warm. Your wages disappear as though you were putting them in pockets filled with holes! ⁷ This is what the LORD of Heaven's Armies says: Look at what's happening to you! ⁸ Now go up into the hills, bring down timber, and rebuild my house. Then I will take pleasure in it and be honored, says the LORD. ⁹ You hoped for rich harvests, but they were poor. And when you brought your harvest home, I blew it away. Why? Because my house lies in ruins, says the LORD of Heaven's Armies, while all of you are busy building your own fine houses. [10] It's because of you that the heavens withhold the dew and the earth produces no crops. [11] I have called for a drought on your fields and hills—a drought to wither the grain and grapes and olive trees and all your other crops, a drought to starve you and your livestock and to ruin everything you have worked so hard to get."

This is the story of God's people who were more concerned about building their own houses than about building, maintaining, or repairing the house of God. In other words, they were more interested in their lives and homes than in the things of God and His house.

What did the Lord tell them to do in verses 5 and 7? _____

_____

Because of their disobedience and their wrong priorities, they were obviously not walking in God's blessings. According to verses 6 and 9 through 11, what was happening in the financial and material areas of their lives? _____

_____

If they wanted to walk in God's blessings, what were they to do, according to verse 8? _____

_____

Can you see any parallels in this story with your own life?

_____

Malachi 3:10

Bring all the tithes into the storehouse so there will be enough food in my Temple. . . .

Where did God tell His people to bring their tithes? _____

_____

How much of the tithe were they supposed to bring to the storehouse? _____

What does the tithe allow the storehouse to provide for God's people? _____

The word "storehouse" in Hebrew is *owtsar* and its meanings include a depository, armory, cellar, store, treasure, treasure house.[1]

Let's dig into this. Many theologians believe this is a reference to the local church. In Old Testament times, the storehouse provided literal food and meat for God's people. In New Testament times, the storehouse of the local church provides spiritual food and meat for God's people.

Notice, all the tithe was supposed to go to the storehouse. In other words, we are to bring the entire ten percent to the storehouse. It is not scriptural to subdivide our tithe and give it to various or multiple ministries. We may give offerings over and above our tithe to various ministries, but the tithe itself belongs in its entirety to the storehouse. (Again, we will talk about offerings in our next lesson.)

Remember the story of the widow's mites? "Jesus sat down near the collection box in the Temple and watched as the crowds dropped in their money. Many rich people put in large amounts. Then a poor widow came and dropped in two small coins. Jesus called his disciples to him and said, 'I tell you the truth, this poor widow has given more than all the others who are making contributions. For they gave a tiny part of their surplus, but she, poor as she is, has given everything she had to live on'" (Mark 12:41-44).

When Jesus sat near the collection box in the temple and watched people returning their tithes and offering to God, He approved of them bringing their gifts to His house. Had He wanted to change their view of bringing gifts to the storehouse, this might have been a great time to say, "Hey everyone, we're going to be setting up some new guidelines for giving. No need to bring your gifts to this local storehouse. Feel free to divvy it up and give to whatever ministries as you feel led. Especially you, little widow mite lady. You barely have enough to live on. Just keep your mites."

The local church you attend is your spiritual storehouse. It is there that God has a depository, a store and treasure house full of ministry, teaching, revelation, opportunity, prayer, care, and love to give you. It is there that God has given you pastors, teachers, and leaders, who teach you and your entire family the Word. Through worship and weekly messages, small groups, Bible schools, and special events, there is a constant buffet of God's Word being dished up in your local church.

At your local church you find the family of God, pastors as well as brothers and sisters in Christ, who minister to your needs and help you in times of distress and trouble. They visit you in the hospital, sit with you in crisis, and bring meals in difficult times. They receive your late-night phone calls and provide godly counsel. They dedicate your babies, marry your children, and perform funerals for your loved ones. They pray for you.

Local churches are truly rich, spiritual treasuries in a community. Not only do healthy churches provide ministry to those within the church, they also focus their outreach efforts on those who are outside of the church.

It is the faithful and regular giving of tithers that keeps local church storehouses strong all around the world. If every Christian was convinced and committed to bringing their tithes into their storehouse on a regular basis, God's Church would be an even stronger force on earth than it already is!

HOW SHOULD WE BRING OUR TITHES?

The most important thing is to bring your tithe to the Lord and His storehouse from a heart of love, gratitude, and faith. It's no wonder the Bible tells us God loves a cheerful giver. It's a joy to give God what belongs to Him. He loves it when we give with gratitude and thankfulness for His goodness in our lives!

TAKE THE "PROVE ME NOW" TEST

We need to look a bit more in Malachi to learn more about the "Prove Me Now" challenge!

Malachi 3:10-12 (KJV)

Bring ye all the tithes into the storehouse, that there may be meat in mine house, and prove me now herewith, saith the LORD of hosts, if I will not open you the windows of heaven, and pour you out a blessing, that there shall not be room enough to receive it. [11] And I will rebuke the devourer for your sakes, and he shall not destroy the fruits of your ground; neither shall your vine cast her fruit before the time in the field, saith the LORD of hosts. [12] And all nations shall call you blessed: for ye shall be a delightsome land, saith the LORD of hosts.

What did God say in verse 10? _____

When it comes to His faithfulness in our financial lives, God wants us to prove Him.

2 Corinthians 9:6-8

Remember this—a farmer who plants only a few seeds will get a small crop. But the one who plants generously will get a generous crop. [7] You must each decide in your heart how much to give. And don't give reluctantly or in response to pressure. "For God loves a person who gives cheerfully." [8] And God will generously provide all you need. Then you will always have everything you need and plenty left over to share with others.

According to verse 7, what type of giver does God love?

_____

Throughout Scripture, you get the idea that the Lord really wants His people to take Him up on entering into the blessing of being generous—especially through giving tithes cheerfully! It's like He's egging us on: "C'mon, try it and see. Prove for yourself and see how good I am! Do it! Do it!" And the crazy thing is so many Christians are like, "Uh, no thanks."

Why is that, I wonder? Maybe we've forgotten how fun it is to live by faith? Perhaps we need to remember that we are not under the law.

God did promise to bless His people greatly under that Old Covenant. Now, under the New Covenant also called the "new and better covenant" (Hebrews 12:24), will He be less interested in demonstrating His generous goodness to those who exercise their faith by tithing?

Let's look at the four blessings God promised to tithers: the windows of heaven are opened, blessings are poured out, our livelihood will be protected and we will be called blessed.

4 BLESSINGS FOR THE TITHER

1. Windows of Heaven Opened

God promises to "open the windows of heaven" for faith-filled tithers. In Genesis 7:11 and 8:2, we get a picture of what it means for the "windows of heaven" to be opened. In the days of Noah, God opened the windows of heaven, and it rained down enough to flood the earth. When God opens His windows, things happen!

I don't believe God intended for us to place our tithe in the offering basket, walk outside, gaze up, and wait for dollar bills to come floating down from the windows of heaven. But I do believe we are to expect the windows of heaven to be opened for us. What does that mean?

Many Bible teachers describe the windows of heaven as windows of opportunity. In other words, when the windows of heaven are opened over our lives, God allows us to see through a window we had not seen through before—opportunities to which we previously had been blinded, open up to us.

I love the way the King James Bible describes this idea in Proverbs 8:12, "I wisdom dwell with prudence, and find out knowledge of witty inventions." I believe that part of the windows of heaven being opened over our lives is God giving us the knowledge of witty inventions. That is, He drops innovative ideas into our hearts to help us experience increase and get wealth. Why not expect God to give you new ideas, new doors of opportunity, and even new inventions that will be a blessing to you and to those around you?

Remember in the "My Story" part of this book, where I told you that as a young Christian, I had $50 to my name and 30 days to come up with $2500 to go to Bible School back in the 80's? (With inflation today, that would be equivalent to needing around $6000.) While at church one night our pastor challenged us to participate in a "Prove Me" offering, so I put my entire net worth of $50 into the offering. Well, let me tell you the rest of the story.

I was driving around my hometown of Lansing, Michigan, one day and heard these words in my spirit, "Fruits and vegetables. Fruits and vegetables." I felt it was the Holy Spirit and instantly knew what He was talking about. You see, when I was a student at Boston University, we'd often go to the city to Quincy Market where they sold all kinds of meat, fish, cheeses, and fresh food. (You have to understand this was back in the day before words like organic, health food, and juice bar were so posh.) At Quincy Market, there were several booths where they sold fresh, cut, ready-to-eat mixed fruit and vegetables with ranch dressing in clear plastic cups. As college kids eating dorm food, we always made a beeline to this booth because it was delish—and cheap!

In my hometown in the mid-80's, there was no such option. If you wanted fresh, cut, ready-to-eat fruit or veggies, you had to buy and cut them up yourself at home. (I know it seems crazy now, because the ability to eat any type of fresh, organic, handfed, custom cut, free range anything is the standard bill of fare everywhere. However, this was not the case in Lansing, Michigan, in the 80's!)

In a flash I thought, *What if I could find a way to make cups of fruit and vegetables, just like I enjoyed in Boston, and sell them to and through convenience stores in Lansing? What if I could do all of this in 30 days and raise the $2500 I needed to go to Bible school?* Great idea, right? Except for the fact that I didn't own a fruit or veggie farm, didn't have a commercial kitchen, didn't know where to get plastic cups and lids, had no idea how to sell to convenience stores, didn't know what the health department rules were, and oh, didn't have any money!

As I pondered this idea, I remembered that I had seen a box truck with "McNamara's Produce" written all over it in the parking lot of the church I belonged to. I thought, *Well, I might as well pretend I heard from God and make a phone call.* So I called McNamara's Produce and said something like this, "Hi, my name is Beth Shepard, and I think I saw your truck in the parking lot at my church, Mount Hope Church. Do any of your employees go to church there? If so, I think I might have a good idea for fruits and vegetables." Then I heard the person who answered the phone cover the mouthpiece and holler, "Mickey, there's someone on the phone that needs to talk to you." (Turns out Mickey was one of the owners.) When Mickey came to the phone, I said, "Hey Mickey, you're so fine you blow my mind, hey Mickey." (Had to throw that in.) Actually, I told Mickey the fruits and vegetables idea, and he said, "You *need* to talk to my wife, Annette. She won't believe this. She's had the same idea for three years and was just waiting on the right timing to do it!"

Needless to say, when Annette and I met, we were giddy! I told her what I had seen at Quincy Market in Boston and that I was leaving for Bible school in less than 30 days and needed $2500 I told her if she thought we could pull off a fruit and veggie business, I would work my tail off cleaning, cutting, packaging, and selling fruit and veggie cups.

She was all in and told me that she would cover all the expenses, provide me with the space to work in their commercial kitchen, and give me all the profits on the sales I could make in the time we had left, to help me get to Bible school. The next morning at the crack of dawn, I was at McNamara's Produce cleaning and cutting up fruits and veggies and by noon, I was pounding the pavement with samples and looking for customers. When I reflect on that season, I almost can't believe it myself, except I was there! The Lord did some remarkable things in that short space of time.

Here's one part of that story I hope will inspire you. Lansing is the state capital of Michigan, and one day while trying to sell the fruit and veggie cups, I drove by several of the state buildings and had this thought, *They have small snack bars and concession stands in every one of their buildings and these fruit and veggie cups would be perfect for them.* As I looked at the various buildings within blocks of each other, I decided to go into the Department of Treasury building (seemed fitting) and when I found the snack bar area, I asked for the manager. It just so happened that not only was the manager in, but the man who oversaw all of the snack bars and concession stands in all of the state buildings was at that snack bar, right then! He gave me five minutes to give my spiel and then he placed a trial order!

When it was time for me to leave for Bible school, Mickey and Annette gave me all the thirty day profits from this endeavor (and I think they kicked in a little extra), and I left for Bible School with the $2500 I needed.

So, what wild, miraculous financial miracle do you need?

2. Blessings Poured Out

Let me tell you another windows-of-heaven-opened-and-blessings-poured-out story to stir up your faith. I remember a flight to Minneapolis, when my husband and I were heading to attend a Pastor's conference. While minding my own business on a Southwest flight, the Lord dropped a witty idea into my heart. The idea was to write a fun, game-type gift book for parties, class reunions, and the like called *The Baby Boomers Little Quiz Book: 150 Questions to Prove You Really Grew Up Wearing Bell-Bottoms.* I grabbed a napkin from the flight attendant and within a few minutes, I began to write simple questions like "What was the dog's name on Johnny Quest?" "What are Red Ball Jets?" "Can you sing all the words to the 'Gilligan's Island' theme song?" "Who was Mrs. Beasley?" and more!

Of course, all Baby Boomers would know the answers to such questions, and a fun book like this would stir up fun memories of their childhoods. It was such a simple idea and the content for the book came so quickly! To be honest, I wasn't sure if this was a God-idea or just my own whim, so I decided to pretend it was a legitimate idea from the Lord and began to take steps to see where it would go. Long story short, I wrote the book and had it printed and over the next several years, the Lord helped it to get into various big box stores and Hallmark outlets. It turned out to be a great learning experience in the world of mass-market publishing and was an additional financial stream for us as well.

How about one more story? This one's about a single mom with two boys. We find her in 2 Kings 4:1-7. She faced a financial crisis, and God opened up the windows of heaven and poured out blessings on her with a new stream of income. Let's look.

2 Kings 4:1-7

One day the widow of a member of the group of prophets came to Elisha and cried out, "My husband who served you is dead, and you know how he feared the LORD. But now a creditor has come, threatening to take my two sons as slaves." ² "What can I do to help you?" Elisha asked. "Tell me, what do you have in the house?" "Nothing at all, except a flask of olive oil," she replied.³ And Elisha said, "Borrow as many empty jars as you can from your friends and neighbors. ⁴ Then go into your house with your sons and shut the door behind you. Pour olive oil from your flask into the jars, setting each one aside when it is filled." ⁵ So she did as she was told. Her sons kept bringing jars to her, and she filled one after another. ⁶ Soon every container was full to the brim! "Bring me another jar," she said to one of her sons. "There aren't any more!" he told her. And then the olive oil stopped flowing.⁷ When she told the man of God what had happened, he said to her, "Now sell the olive oil and pay your debts, and you and your sons can live on what is left over."

This is one of my favorite stories in the Bible because it's a story of hope, faith, and the entrepreneurial spirit that resulted in wealth and generosity. The widow had to answer four questions, and so do we: What do you want? What do you have? What will you do? Why will you do it?

What do you want? The widow wanted to save her kids from the creditors, and this deep desire was her motivating force. What is your deep desire? What do you want?

What do you have? The widow didn't have much, but what she did have—a pot of oil—God was able to use. What things, skills, experience, expertise, success, or talents do you have?

What will you do? The widow borrowed containers from others and poured out what she had into the vessels, and God touched and multiplied her oil! But it didn't stop there. Once she had a garage full of oil inventory, she had to get out of her comfort zone and sell the oil. You can borrow ideas, methods, and inspiration from others and begin pouring what you have into those frameworks. Once God touches and multiplies what you have, you'll have to get busy marketing, selling, and monetizing.

Why will you do it? The widow made a lot of money, paid her debts, and she and her boys went to Disneyland! The Lord can help you make a lot of money so you can pay your debts and enjoy life with your loved ones, too. On top of that, you can make a huge contribution to paying a gospel debt and financing your church, ministries, missionaries, and other agencies that are taking the gospel to a needy world.

God has additional streams of income for you, dear friend. You can be sure that God is good, generous, and eager to multiply whatever we give to Him and for Him. Isn't that what Jesus said in Luke 6:38 (KJV), "Give, and it shall be given unto you; good measure, pressed down, and shaken together, and running over, shall men give into your bosom." Blessings are running over! As a tither, you have every right to expect God's blessings will be running all over your life!

3. Livelihood Protected

God said He would guard our crops (the source of our income) from destruction. This means Satan cannot destroy that which produces income for the tither. In addition, it sounds like Satan cannot destroy that which your income has purchased. Have you ever noticed that for those who tithe, their vocations and even their material possessions like cars, tires, toasters, computers, TVs, washing machines, clothing, and all kinds of other material things seem to last longer and don't break down as often as normal? God rebukes the devourer for the sake of the tither!

We've heard interesting stories about how the Lord rebuked the devourer and protected the lives and possessions of tithers. He certainly did for the Israelites in the wilderness. Their clothes and shoes didn't wear out for forty years! (Deuteronomy 29:5; Nehemiah 9:21.) He did the same thing for Mr. Alexander Kerr, founder of the Kerr Glass Jar Company.

An article by Perry Stone relays this story: "Kerr was converted to Christ at age 14 under the ministry of D.L. Moody and later joined the Presbyterian Church in Philadelphia. In 1902, he read Judah's Scepter and Joseph's Birthright, where Jacob had nothing and vowed to tithe to God. Twenty years later, Jacob returned with so much wealth that he was giving it away. On June 1, 1902, Kerr vowed to God that he would set aside a percentage of his income for God's work. At that time, he had a mortgage on his home, owed bills and was burdened with many cares, but had a firm faith in God. After just three months, unexpected blessings began to flow into his business and he started a jar factory to produce Kerr glass jars, with the factory located in San Francisco, California.

"On April 18, 1906, the infamous San Francisco earthquake struck with a magnitude of 7.8 to 8.25, with the greatest damage in San Francisco. It took 3,000 lives and caused damage comparable to Hurricane Katrina. Kerr was out of state when he received a wire that the earthquake had struck, the city was burning, and buildings had fallen. People who were with Kerr told him, 'You are a ruined man, Mr. Kerr.' Kerr is said to have replied, 'I am only ruined if God is. I don't believe it, or the Bible is not true. God will not go back on his promises!'

"The Kerr factory was a two-story wood building with huge tanks where glass was melted. The tanks were kept at 2,500 degrees and oil was used for fuel, so this building should have been the most flammable. Kerr later examined his building and saw where the fire had burned outside the wooden fence, but never scorched the inside of the fence. To his amazement, not one jar was broken! In 1912, he began placing in each case of jars a leaflet called 'God's Cure for Poverty,' which revealed the power of the covenant of giving." [2]

4. Blessings Seen

Another blessing is being seen as blessed by others. God says that all nations shall call you blessed, for you will be a land of delight (Malachi 3:12). I believe God wants others to see His blessings in our lives. Joy, peace, loving relationships, wealth, and increase preaches a wonderful message about the goodness of God. As we share the blessings God has given to us with others, we preach a sermon people around us can understand!

Many times, the world around us doesn't see us in our prayer closets. They don't see us attending church. They don't see us reading our Bibles, praising the Lord, or wearing a "halo." But they do see our lifestyle and generosity, and one thing the world can recognize is wealth and generosity.

COMMON QUESTIONS

As we wrap up this session, let's answer a few common questions.

1. Didn't Jesus say we shouldn't talk about giving and that it should be kept secret?

Should we talk about money? Should giving always be kept secret? These are great questions.

Jesus did say, "Watch out! Don't do your good deeds publicly, to be admired by others, for you will lose the reward from your Father in heaven. When you give to someone in need, don't do as the hypocrites do—blowing trumpets in the synagogues and streets to call attention to their acts of charity! I tell you the truth, they have received all the reward they will ever get. But when you give to someone in need, don't let your left hand know what your right hand is doing. Give your gifts in private, and your Father, who sees everything, will reward you" (Matthew 6:1-4).

What was Jesus talking about? Randy Alcorn, bestselling author of 27 books, including *Money, Possessions and Eternity* and *The Treasure Principle,* brings out the fact that in this passage, Jesus was dealing with motives.

> This is not a prohibition against others becoming aware of our giving, prayers, fasting, Bible study, feeding the poor, missions work, or church attendance. Rather, it's a command not to do these things in order to receive the recognition of men. Jesus continues, "If you do [that is, if you do good things to win human approval], you will have no reward from your Father in heaven." The problem isn't doing good things with reward in mind—it's looking for the reward from men rather than from

God … This is a figure of speech. It's hyperbole, a deliberate overstatement, which would have been immediately clear to the hearers. That Christ's command cannot be literal is self-evident, because a hand lacks the ability to know anything, and besides the person's brain would know what both the right hand and the left hand were doing. So what's Christ's point? Do your giving quietly, unobtrusively. Don't cough loudly just as you're giving. Drop your check in the offering or send it in the mail without drawing attention to yourself. Give in a spirit of humility and simplicity, as an act of worship. Don't give in order to get your name on a list. Don't dwell on your gift, fixating on it. Building a mental shrine to yourself. In other words, don't make a big production out of it, either in view of others or in the privacy of your own heart. But can this verse mean it's always wrong for others to know that we've given? No. Acts 2:45 tells of Christians selling possessions and giving to the needy. These people knew each other. If you no longer had your prize camels, coat, or oxcart, and Caleb ben Judah did, people would figure it out. Acts 4:32-35 tells us about more people liquidating assets. Most names, which would mean nothing to us, aren't recorded, but they were surely known at the time. But some givers were named even for our benefit… The risks of disclosing a person's giving are sometimes outweighed by the benefits of disclosure. If Christ established a principle in Matthew 6:2-4 that other people should never know what someone gives, then the members of the early Church violated it in Acts 4:36-37. There's no way around it.

Let's look at this dichotomy. In Acts 4:36-37, we find out what Barnabas gave. He sold a field and gave the funds to the apostles. His testimony of giving was an inspiration for others.

Acts 4:36-37

For instance, there was Joseph, the one the apostles nicknamed Barnabas (which means "Son of Encouragement"). He was from the tribe of Levi and came from the island of Cyprus. [37] He sold a field he owned and brought the money to the apostles.

In Acts 5:1-11, we find out what Ananias and Sapphira gave. In their case, they lied and their motives were completely wrong. The result in their case? They died!

Acts 5:1-11

But there was a certain man named Ananias who, with his wife, Sapphira, sold some property. [2] He brought part of the money to the apostles, claiming it was the full amount. With his wife's consent, he kept the rest. [3] Then Peter said, "Ananias, why have you let Satan fill your heart? You lied to the Holy Spirit, and you kept some of the money for yourself. [4] The property was yours to sell or not sell, as you wished. And after selling it, the money was also yours to give away. How could you do a thing like this? You weren't lying to us but to God!" [5] As soon as Ananias heard these words, he fell to the floor and died. Everyone who heard about it was terrified. [6] Then some young men got up, wrapped him in a sheet, and took him out and buried him. [7] About three hours later his wife came in, not knowing what had happened. [8] Peter asked her, "Was this the price you and your husband received for your land?" "Yes," she replied, "that was the price." [9] And Peter said, "How could the two of you even think of conspiring to test the Spirit of the Lord like this? The young men who buried your husband are just outside the door, and they will carry you out, too." [10] Instantly, she fell to the floor and died. When the young men came in and saw that she was dead, they carried her out and buried her beside her husband. [11] Great fear gripped the entire church and everyone else who heard what had happened.

In other accounts in the Bible, we are told exactly what people gave in various offerings. So, when a person's heart and motives are pure, it must be okay with the Lord to share these things. Check out Numbers 7 to see the lists of donors and their specific gifts made to the tabernacle.

In 1 Chronicles 29:2-9, we find out exactly what King David and the leadership team gave to build the temple

"Using every resource at my command, I have gathered as much as I could for building the Temple of my God. Now there is enough gold, silver, bronze, iron, and wood, as well as great quantities of onyx, other precious stones, costly jewels, and all kinds of fine stone and marble. [3] And now, because of my devotion to the Temple of my God, I am giving all of my own private treasures of gold and silver to help in the construction. This is in addition to the building materials I have already collected for his holy Temple. [4] I am donating more than 112 tons of gold from Ophir and 262 tons of refined silver to be used for overlaying the walls of the buildings [5] and for the other gold and silver work to be done by the craftsmen. Now then, who will follow my example and give offerings to the LORD today?" [6] Then the family leaders, the leaders of the tribes of Israel, the generals and captains of the army, and the king's administrative officers all gave willingly. [7] For the construction of the Temple of God, they gave about 188 tons of gold, 10,000 gold coins,

375 tons of silver, 675 tons of bronze, and 3,750 tons of iron. [8] They also contributed numerous precious stones, which were deposited in the treasury of the house of the LORD under the care of Jehiel, a descendant of Gershon. [9] The people rejoiced over the offerings, for they had given freely and wholeheartedly to the LORD, and King David was filled with joy.

Often, the example of one believer's generous giving can be an inspiration to others to step up in their own giving and measure of generosity. When our motives for giving are not to be seen of men but to honor God, sharing the testimony after our giving for the glory of God and as an example for others seems consistent with the Scriptures. After all, Jesus said, "Let your light so shine before men, that they may see your good works and glorify your Father in heaven" (Matthew 5:16). Remember, Hebrews 10:24 tells us to "spur one another on toward love and good deeds," and our giving can serve as a model for this very thing.

I don't know about you, but I am so challenged and inspired when I hear of the generous giving of others that it encourages me to raise the bar, think bigger, give more generously, and expand my faith in God!

2. Isn't God concerned more with our motives and contentment than with our finanacial status?

The Lord is certainly interested in our motives and contentment, but not to the exclusion of our financial wellbeing. It's not an either-or proposition. When our hearts are in the right place, we can and should have pure motives, a content heart, and absolute freedom to get wealth and be generous. Believers with these traits are a wonderful breed! In fact, 2 Chronicles 16:9 (KJV) hints that God is looking for these types of people: "For the eyes of the Lord run to and fro throughout the whole earth, to show Himself strong on behalf of those whose heart is loyal to Him."

First Timothy 6:6 tells us, "Yet true godliness with contentment is itself great wealth," and Hebrews 13:5, says, "Don't love money; be satisfied with what you have. For God has said, 'I will never fail you. I will never abandon you.'"

There is something rich and right about pursuing godliness and being content with our lot in life. At the same time, it's perfectly acceptable to believe God and His promises concerning getting wealth and establishing His covenant.

3. What about people who don't tithe but seem to be blessed and prosperous?

Ever feel like everyone else is living the dream—especially your friends on Instagram?

The psalmist had a very similar question. No matter what happens or doesn't happen in given seasons of our lives, it's always good to keep things in perspective. Let's see what we can learn about perspective from his experience in Psalm 73—pay particular attention to verses 16-17.

Psalm 73

Truly God is good to Israel,
to those whose hearts are pure.
2 But as for me, I almost lost my footing.
My feet were slipping, and I was almost gone.
3 For I envied the proud
when I saw them prosper despite their wickedness.

⁴ They seem to live such painless lives;

their bodies are so healthy and strong.

⁵ They don't have troubles like other people;

they're not plagued with problems like everyone else.

⁶ They wear pride like a jeweled necklace

and clothe themselves with cruelty.

⁷ These fat cats have everything

their hearts could ever wish for!

⁸ They scoff and speak only evil;

in their pride they seek to crush others.

⁹ They boast against the very heavens,

and their words strut throughout the earth.

¹⁰ And so the people are dismayed and confused,

drinking in all their words.

¹¹ "What does God know?" they ask.

"Does the Most High even know what's happening?"

¹² Look at these wicked people—

enjoying a life of ease while their riches multiply.

¹³ Did I keep my heart pure for nothing?

Did I keep myself innocent for no reason?

¹⁴ I get nothing but trouble all day long;

every morning brings me pain.

¹⁵ If I had really spoken this way to others,

I would have been a traitor to your people.

¹⁶ So I tried to understand why the wicked prosper.

But what a difficult task it is!

¹⁷ Then I went into your sanctuary, O God,

and I finally understood the destiny of the wicked.

¹⁸ Truly, you put them on a slippery path

and send them sliding over the cliff to destruction.

[19] In an instant they are destroyed,

completely swept away by terrors.

[20] When you arise, O Lord,

you will laugh at their silly ideas

as a person laughs at dreams in the morning.

[21] Then I realized that my heart was bitter,

and I was all torn up inside.

[22] I was so foolish and ignorant—

I must have seemed like a senseless animal to you.

[23] Yet I still belong to you;

you hold my right hand.

[24] You guide me with your counsel,

leading me to a glorious destiny.

[25] Whom have I in heaven but you?

I desire you more than anything on earth.

[26] My health may fail, and my spirit may grow weak,

but God remains the strength of my heart;

he is mine forever.

[27] Those who desert him will perish,

for you destroy those who abandon you.

[28] But as for me, how good it is to be near God!

I have made the Sovereign LORD my shelter,

and I will tell everyone about the wonderful things you do.

LET'S GET PRACTICAL

I know we've covered a lot of ground, and you have a lot to get excited about! Just remember, the ability to tithe is a blessing to be received, not an obligation or duty. Here are two practical ways to implement what we've studied:

1) Trust God and make a decision to be a tither. Whenever you get paid or receive any extra income or increase, settle in your heart that from now on, the first ten percent belongs to the Lord.

2) Set up your plan for giving your tithes to your local church. Many churches offer options for giving, whether by cash, check, automatic deduction, texting, online giving, and more. Decide on the best way to give consistently, and get started with your next paycheck.

When we give God our first ten percent, it seems to set apart our remaining ninety percent as blessed! I hope you will begin to tithe and enter into the blessed flow God has in store for you!

I love this quote from the late Adrian Rogers: "You'll always do more with nine-tenths and God as a partner, than you do with ten-tenths by yourself. It's time we began to trust the Lord!"

JOURNAL ENTRY

To get the most out of this chapter, take a few moments to journal your thoughts and/or prayers.

_____

_____

_____

_____

_____

_____

_____

_____

_____

_____

_____

_____

_____

_____

_____

_____

_____

SESSION 3
THE MULTIPLIED FRUIT
OF OFFERINGS

———❖———

"**S**eriously? They're asking me to give more money? I already tithe. Now, they want me to give offerings, too? They're about to make me a *nillionaire*!" As a young Christian, I remember being in various church services or Christian conferences and being bugged by this whole notion of giving more than your tithe. I wondered if I would have any money left by the time I gave into every offering bucket that was passed my way. (Can I get an "Amen," dear reader?) That is, until I received revelation knowledge on the partnership God was inviting me to join. Until that time, I viewed giving as a bogus situation where God and everyone else won and I lost. (Yeah, as a massive giver, I was deeply concerned about losing my $10.)

In my mind, all types of giving were under one umbrella. I didn't realize the Bible said so much about the different types of giving and the blessings associated with them. I knew Malachi was "the tithing passage," but I never noticed its reference to offerings: "Will a man rob God? Yet you have robbed Me! But you say, 'In what way have we robbed You?' In tithes and *offerings*" (Malachi 3:8, NKJV). That was in the Old Testament, but when I traveled into the New Testament, I was struck by the hundreds of references to words like give, gave, giving, generous, generously, generosity, not to mention, tithe, tithes, offering and alms.

I thought, *Holy smokes, God takes this whole giving thing seriously. Perhaps, I should, too!* One thing that helped me was seeing the distinction God makes between tithes and offerings. When I saw them as two different things, and then giving alms to the poor as something else (hold onto your hat, we'll cover alms in Session 4), it made sense to me and stirred up my desire to get involved in God's economy of generosity.

So, let's dig into this subject and start by looking at the difference between tithes and offerings. These distinctions helped me. I hope they help you.

As we saw in our last session, the tithe represents ten percent of our income. The tithe belongs to the Lord. The tithe is *not* a seed; it is holy and the first fruit we give to God. We give our tithes to God's storehouse, the local church. As tithers, we can have absolute confidence that God will bless our remaining ninety percent in such a way that we won't even miss the ten percent tithe we gave back to Him.

When it comes to offerings, these are financial gifts of any amount over and above our tithe. Offerings belong to us. Offerings are our discretionary funds and are considered to be seeds. We are able to sow offerings as financial seeds into any field (people, places, or things) as we desire and as the Holy Spirit prompts us to plant. God promised we will reap what we sow. This is where it gets fun!

OFFERINGS ARE FINANCIAL SEEDS

In addition to agricultural seeds, the Bible specifically tells us about at least two types of seeds:

1) Spiritual Seeds: Sowing the seed of the Word of God into our hearts enables us to reap spiritual harvests of thirty-, sixty-, and one hundred-fold (Mark 4:13-20).

2) Financial Seeds: Sowing financial seeds into good ground through the law of sowing and reaping (sometimes called the law of seed-time and harvest or the principle of investment and increase), gives everyone a fair opportunity to become a "financial farmer" and reap eternal and financial rewards (2 Corinthians 9:6).

Let's look at this concept of seedtime and harvest.

Genesis 8:22 (NKJV)

While the earth remains, seedtime and harvest, cold and heat, winter and summer, and day and night shall not cease.

What does God say will not cease as long as the earth remains?

_____

Genesis 1:11-12, 29-30 (NKJV)

Then God said, "Let the earth bring forth grass, the herb *that* yields seed, and the fruit tree *that* yields fruit according to its kind, whose seed is in itself, on the earth"; and it was so. ¹² And the earth brought forth grass, the herb *that* yields seed according to its kind, and the tree *that* yields fruit, whose seed *is* in itself according to its kind. And God saw that *it was* good. . . ²⁹ And

God said, "See, I have given you every herb *that* yields seed which *is* on the face of all the earth, and every tree whose fruit yields seed; to you it shall be for food. [30] Also, to every beast of the earth, to every bird of the air, and to everything that creeps on the earth, in which *there is* life, *I have given* every green herb for food"; and it was so.

God set "seedtime and harvest" in motion at Creation.

What does God say the seeds in the herb and fruit will produce?

_____

What does the phrase, "the seed is in itself" mean to you?

_____

In creation, we see God instituting the law of the seed in plants, in animals, and in mankind. The seed that was in every herb, every fruit tree, and every creature that God created was designed to produce after its kind. In every apple, there are five seeds. If you plant those seeds, they each contain the potential to multiply exponentially by producing five apple trees that produce hundreds of apples, each with five seeds, and on it goes. The seed for whatever we need is within itself!

In other words, if you need more dollar bills, there are seeds in a one dollar bill. Plant that dollar bill into good ground as the Spirit leads you, and in a season or two, that dollar will produce a dollar tree that produces dollar bills. Each of those new dollars have seeds within them, and on it goes! (Whoa! Turns out money grows on trees after all!)

Can you see this, friends? For example, not only would the seed of the fruit tree produce a particular fruit, the fruit would have within it more seeds that would produce more fruit that had seed in it "after his kind," continually perpetuating itself. So if you have a seed, you have the potential for a harvest, baby!

Let's look at what the Word of God says about this matter of sowing and reaping money.

2 Corinthians 9:1-15

I really don't need to write to you about this ministry of giving for the believers in Jerusalem. [2] For I know how eager you are to help, and I have been boasting to the churches in Macedonia that you in Greece were ready to send an offering a year ago. In fact, it was your enthusiasm that stirred up many of the Macedonian believers to begin giving. [3] But I am sending these brothers to be sure you really are ready, as I have been telling them, and that your money is all collected. I don't want to be wrong in my boasting about you. [4] We would be embarrassed—not to mention your own embarrassment—if some Macedonian believers came with me and found that you weren't ready after all I had told them! [5] So I thought I should send these brothers ahead of me to make sure the gift you promised is ready. But I want it to be a willing gift, not one given grudgingly. [6] Remember this—a farmer who plants only a few seeds will get a small crop. But the one who plants generously will get a generous crop. [7] You must each decide in your heart how much to give. And don't give reluctantly or in response to pressure. "For God loves a person who gives cheerfully." [8] And God will generously provide all you need. Then you will always have everything you need and plenty left over to share with others. [9] As the Scriptures say, "They share freely and give generously to the poor. Their good deeds will be remembered forever." [10] For God is the one who provides seed for the farmer and then bread to eat. In the same way, he will provide and increase your resources and then produce a great harvest of generosity in you. [11] Yes, you will be enriched in every way so that you can always be generous. And when we take your gifts to those who need them, they will thank God. [12] So two good things will result from this ministry of giving—the needs of the believers in Jerusalem will be met, and they will joyfully express their thanks to God. [13] As a result of your ministry, they will give glory to God. For your generosity to them and to all believers will prove that you are obedient to the Good News of Christ. [14] And they will pray for you with deep affection because of the overflowing grace God has given to you. [15] Thank God for this gift too wonderful for words!

This passage deals specifically with the subject of financial giving. The believers in Macedonia had been generous in giving to the poor saints in Jerusalem, and Paul was commending and instructing them. He included a reference to God's law of sowing and reaping right in the middle of these passages on financial giving!

The law of seedtime and harvest is an interesting one because we reap exactly what we sow. The seed will produce after its kind. In the natural, if you sow corn, you will reap corn; if you sow beans, you will reap beans. In spiritual matters, if you sow mercy, you will reap mercy; if you sow love and kindness, you will reap love and kindness. If you sow material things, you can expect to reap material things. If you sow finances, you will reap finances. The seed always produces after its kind! We can't sow corn and expect to reap beans. We can't sow hatred and expect to reap love. By the same token, we can't expect to reap finances by sowing corn. Whatever we desire to reap is exactly what we must sow!

Let's take a look at this in more detail.

This whole chapter is talking about sowing generous financial offering seeds. Let's see what we can learn.

According to verse 6, if we only plant a few seeds, what can we expect? _____

If we plant a generous number of seeds, what can we expect?

_____

According to verse 7, who decides what we should give? _____

_____

What type of giver does God love? _____

According to verse 8, what will God provide? _____

_____

According to verse 10, to whom does God give seed? _____

_____

According to verses 10-11, what does God provide and enrich?

_____

From verses 12-15, list all of the things that God says will result through sowing generous financial seeds. _____

_____

Every word in this passage is loaded with life and faith for being generous and reaping God's goodness! As we sow our financial seeds, not only will we be blessed with a bountiful return on our sowing, but God will also use our seed to bless others. Our seed multiplies to bless those to whom we give it, and we also receive an increase on our seed. God's economy is a win-win situation for everyone who will cooperate with His plan!

In this session, I am going to share a little more of our financial journey. I am doing this, not so you'll be impressed (or unimpressed) with us, but so you'll have an increased confidence in God. Besides, our wealth and generosity experience might sound like chump change to those who far out give us. To others, perhaps our experience will inspire you to raise the bar on your own giving. Either way, the whole goal is to increase your faith and turn your eyes to God's faithfulness, His goodness, and the joy of sowing financial seeds into good ground!

I remember a season in our young and growing family's life when it became apparent that we needed a huge increase in our finances. We needed furniture, a bigger car, and we wanted to feed hungry children (our four!). Plus, our kids were beginning to get involved in sports and needed all the gear (which only costs a small fortune). On top of that, we knew that as they got older, things like braces, cars, and college tuition would be our new normal, so our expenses were only going to go up. At the time, we were pioneering a small church, so a pay increase that would meet our needs was not in the foreseeable future. The truth is, we secretly wished some rich financial farmers would have a midnight vision from the angel Gabriel and hear words like, "Behold, I bring you glad tidings, you should sow financial seeds into your pastors' lives and take all the pressure off of them. . . ." Instead, we heard things like, "Behold, that's not how it works! If you want to reap generously, you go ahead and sow generously." #yourseedisinyourneed

One day while looking out our back window, I stared at the twenty-acre plot of farmland behind our house and pondered the process it must have taken that farmer to go from planting one corn seed to now planting thousands of seeds to load his twenty-acre plot of land. I wondered if he started by planting one acre the first year, and then as those crops came in, he used the seed from that harvest to sow into two acres the next year and five acres the next year and on and on until he had enough seed to sow into and reap from all twenty acres.

It hit me that day! We needed a *twenty-acre increase* in our financial crops. If we would get started by sowing the financial seeds we had into one acre of ministry, then as those financial crops came in, we could use the seeds from that harvest to sow into two more acres of ministry, and then eventually, we'd have continual seed to sow into twenty acres, and this would result in loads of financial harvest and more seeds to sow! Eventually, we could get to the twenty-acre increase we needed. I realized that this would not happen overnight. Just like good farmers, we would have to be patient as our crops increased. It made perfect sense in my mind.

My husband and I decided to see what kind of financial seed we had available so we could get busy sowing it. Turns out we were eating all of our seed to survive. We literally didn't have any seed to sow, or so we thought. However, as we just saw in the prior passage, "He supplies seed to the sower" (2 Corinthians 9:10, NKJV), we knew we needed to get bold and creative.

Here's what we did. At that time, we really needed a larger car for our family, but instead of taking on a monthly car payment and expenses, we decided to wait on the car and chose to sow the $500 we would have spent each month for our payment, insurance, and gas into *five acres of ministry*. We prayed and felt inclined to sow $500 per month (that was huge for us!); this meant $100/month into five different gospel-preaching ministries for one year. We also decided that any unexpected funds that came into our lives that year would be considered *seed to sow*, and we would plant those funds into whomever and wherever as the Lord led us. We became a seed-sowing factory that year, and do you know what happened? At first, not much. (Other than when we found money under the sofa cushions or in the pockets of clothing in the dryer, we considered it the beginning of our harvest!) We had to exercise patience. But over the next several years, we entered a cycle of sowing and reaping, and bigger crops started to come in.

It had begun; our five acres of sowing was turning into twenty acres of seedtime and harvest! From that point on, we have continued to sow financial seeds, as well as things like clothing, jewelry, motorcycles, vehicles and "stuff" into more acreage (people, ministries, churches, and gospel initiatives), and we have continued to reap multiplied crops according to the measure we have sown.

The funny thing is, just when we got comfortable with our personal level of sowing and reaping, God challenged us to raise our giving by hundreds and thousands of dollars at a time. Now, mind you, it's not like we had buckets of money lying around, but we had seen enough of God's faithfulness to His principles of seedtime and harvest at work, that we want to stay hooked up to His economic flow!

Recently, my husband and I were talking about God's faithfulness to give us harvest upon harvest and increased seed to sow over the years! From being a taker for the first few years of my Christian life, to becoming a giver with the first $50 "Prove Me Now" offering I sowed way back when I first learned about giving, to eventually tithing and now being led by the Lord to gladly sow financial gifts into people and ministries that have impacted us—giving has truly become a fun, sowing and reaping adventure for my husband and I.

Here are a few stories that I hope inspire you to believe God for bigger things in your own life of sowing and reaping.

Church building campaigns always have a way of revealing where the treasures of our hearts lie. When we built our first church building in the 90's, the Lord prompted us to lead the way for our congregation by giving a $10,000 cash offering and making an additional $20,000 pledge to the building fund. This was significantly more than we'd ever given before—but as soon as we committed to giving, we experienced great joy and expectation. And, of course, God was faithful and His laws of seedtime and harvest went into motion.

Years later, in 2008 when the world's economy was collapsing and going into a recession, our church purchased 30 acres of land on the major highway between Detroit and Chicago and we prepared to build a large new facility that would enable our church to reach more people in Southwest Michigan. The faith-stretching part is that during this global financial crisis, the Lord led us to sow $50,000—the largest seed we'd ever given—into the new building and campus expansion. It was such a crazy financial time, we literally laughed out loud as we made our commitment. And wouldn't you know, in ways only God can orchestrate, the biggest harvests we'd ever seen began pouring into our lives as well.

But then—here's the mind-blowing part—a few years later, the Lord challenged us to sow an even larger seed—a house! (It might sound crazy to some, but we knew from experience that whenever God asked us to sow something extravagant, it's because He has something more extravagant He wants us to reap!)

You see in the early 2000s, the Lord led us to buy a rental home in a booming area of Florida. Over the years, our equity in the home had grown to over $100,000. That's when we sensed the Lord wanted us to donate the home and the $100,000 in equity to a gospel endeavor. That was a huge milestone and a great joy for us! God has been beyond faithful in multiplying our seed and giving us harvest after harvest.

Sometimes, we have to pinch ourselves when we think about how far the Lord has brought us. I had no idea what God had in store for our lives when He challenged me to prove Him in giving $50 away, but we are living proof—God is faithful.

And, dear friends, He will be faithful to you, too!

Galatians 6:7-10

Don't be misled—you cannot mock the justice of God. You will always harvest what you plant. [8] Those who live only to satisfy their own sinful nature will harvest decay and death from that sinful nature. But those who live to please the Spirit will harvest everlasting life from the Spirit. [9] So let's not get tired of doing what is good. At just the right time we will reap a harvest of blessing if we don't give up. [10] Therefore, whenever we have the opportunity, we should do good to everyone—especially to those in the family of faith.

What will a person always harvest? _____

If we sow selfishly to our sinful desires, what will we reap?

_____

If we sow unselfishly to the Spirit's desire, what will we reap?

_____

When will we reap a harvest? _____

Who should we intentionally sow goodness into? _____

_____

Let's revisit an important reality. Sowing and reaping require patience. Every time we have sown finances into the kingdom of God, we've had to exercise faith and patience and not cast away our confidence. But God will not be mocked. As I have shared, we have reaped what we have sown in "due season."

There have been occasions when we have sown financial seed by faith and have seen the increase immediately, and there have been times when the harvest has come in slowly. The most difficult thing to do after you've sown is to not give up, stay in faith, and faint not because in due season, you will reap!

Several years ago, the Lord put it on my heart to give away my car. It was a loaded Lexus that we had fully paid off. (Getting the car to begin with was a God-story in and of itself!) I had driven it for about six years when the Lord put it in my heart to give it to a pastor's wife. I was so excited but just didn't know which pastor's wife! After praying about who should get the car, the Lord put a local pastor's wife on my heart. It was such a joy to surprise her with the car. She was happy about it and a bit in shock. I had so much fun getting the car prepped to give her, and I was elated and beside myself on the day of the big give. Truly, it's more blessed to give than to receive! I discovered that, unbeknownst to me, this pastor's wife had been going through a very difficult season. Turns out that the Lexus was God's way of reminding her that He knew her name and loved her greatly.

You might wonder, what happened to me? Did a brand new Lexus show up in my driveway the next week or the week after that? No! The Lord simply asked me, "What do you want?" I told Him I really wanted a four-door Jeep Wrangler Sahara with a removable top. (I know, some of you are like, "Seriously, God asked you what you wanted and you said a Jeep?" Hey, don't be a hater.) Did He drop one down from the heavens? No. But, several months after the give-away, for the first time in the 20-year history of our church, our Board of Trustees decided to give me a car allowance, and I went out and leased a Jeep. I loved that Jeep! Giving my car away wasn't about getting a nicer car or trying to impress anyone with a new car, it was really a matter of getting to work together with the Lord on the fun adventure of generous living; and in due season, I reaped the exact car I desired. (And, once the Jeep lease was up, I was able to get another car that fulfilled my desire.)

Ecclesiastes 11:4

Farmers who wait for perfect weather never plant. If they watch every cloud, they never harvest.

What type of person will not plant, sow, harvest, or reap? _____

_____

What do you learn from this verse? _____

_____

_____

Did you know that the conditions won't always seem conducive to sowing? In fact, sometimes it'll feel like you're having an "out of money experience." You won't just happen to have an extra $1000 of seeds in your pocket to plant. Don't be moved by the winds of life or by the clouds that cast shadows. By faith, determine that you will sow and reap according to God's law of seedtime and harvest!

Let's look at ways to sow offering seeds.

4 WAYS TO SOW OFFERING SEEDS

1. Sow Offering Seeds Toward God

Proverbs 3:9-10 (NKJV)

Honor the LORD with your possessions, and with the firstfruits of all your increase; so your barns will be filled with plenty, and your vats will overflow with new wine.

What are you to honor the Lord with? _____

What type of possessions do you have? _____

How would you define the "firstfruits of all your increase"?

_____

How do you define honoring the Lord with these things? _____

_____

Are you honoring the Lord with your possessions and with the firstfruits of all your increase? _____

How could you do better in this area? _____

According to verse 10, what is the result of honoring God with your wealth?_____

When you honor the Lord with your wealth, He promises to fill your barns with plenty!

Luke 12:15-21 (NKJV)

And He said to them, "Take heed and beware of covetousness, for one's life does not consist in the abundance of the things he possesses."[16] Then He spoke a parable to them, saying: "The ground of a certain rich man yielded plentifully. [17] And he thought within himself, saying, 'What shall I do, since I have no room to store my crops?' [18] So he said, 'I will do this: I will pull down my barns and build greater, and there I will store all my crops and my goods. [19] And I will say to my soul, "Soul, you have many goods laid up for many years; take your ease; eat, drink, and be merry."'[20] But God said to him, 'Fool! This night your soul will be required of you; then whose will those things be which you have provided?'[21] So is he who lays up treasure for himself, and is not rich toward God."

Who did the rich man focus his treasures on? _____

Who was he not rich towards? _____

What did God call this man? _____

What happened to this man? _____

2. Sow Offering Seeds into Your Parents

Ephesians 6:1-3 (NKJV)

Children, obey your parents in the Lord, for this is right. [2] "Honor your father and mother," which is the first commandment with promise: [3] "that it may be well with you and you may live long on the earth."

What are we commanded to do toward our parents? _____

_____

In your own words, what are some ways a person could honor his parents? _____

Mark 7:9-13 (NKJV)

He said to them, "*All* too well you reject the commandment of God, that you may keep your tradition. [10] For Moses said, 'Honor your father and your mother'; and, 'He who curses father or mother, let him be put to death.'[11] But you say, 'If a man says to his father or mother, "Whatever profit you might have received from me is Corban"—' (that is, a gift to God), [12] then you no longer let him do anything for his father or his mother, [13] making the word of God of no effect through your tradition which you have handed down. And many such things you do."

Jesus rebuked His followers because they weren't honoring their fathers and mothers as God had commanded. It's interesting to note that in honoring parents, Jesus is clearly making a reference to honoring them by taking care of them financially.

What is Jesus talking about in verse 11? _____

_____

How are we to honor our parents? _____

How are we to honor our parents financially? _____

_____

The Pharisees and scribes taught the people that if a son or daughter told his or her parents, "It is Corban" (which in modern language means, "Sorry, Mom and Dad, I can't help you out financially because I'm giving all my money to God"), then those children would be free from their duty to honor their parents in a financial way. Jesus rebuked this type of thinking, saying that they made the Word of God of no effect by their traditions! In other words, Jesus implied that, as sons and daughters, believers do have an obligation to honor their parents by assisting them financially. (The Holy Spirit inspired the apostle Paul to write the same thing about children and their widowed parents in 1 Timothy 5:4,16.)

In other words, it is pleasing to God when we honor our parents by blessing them financially. What trip have your parents always wanted to take? Can you make it happen for them? How much do they owe on their home? Could you pay off the rest of their mortgage? How are they set for their golden years? Is there a special gift, piece of jewelry, or toy they've always wanted? Maybe now is the time to help them realize that dream.

One of the best things my sisters and I did was let our parents know in advance that when they turned 60, we wanted to celebrate their birthdays by taking each of them on a cruise with us girls, and we did just that. Not only did they have a great time, they also enjoyed knowing ahead of time so they could get excited about their trips long before they happened. Is there a special trip either of your parents would like to take with you?

Many years ago when my mom retired and moved to Florida, she had a beautiful new home but no funds left over for her landscaping. At the time, we had a few thousand dollars in a rainy day fund we planned to use when needed, but one day the Lord just dropped the thought into our hearts to cover the costs so she could get her yard beautifully landscaped. She was thrilled, and it was a joy for us to make this happen for her. What could you make happen for your parents?

3. Sow Offering Seeds into Your Family

Proverbs 31:10-31

[10]Who can find a virtuous and capable wife? She is more precious than rubies. [11] Her husband can trust her, and she will

greatly enrich his life. [12] She brings him good, not harm, all the days of her life. [13] She finds wool and flax and busily spins it. [14] She is like a merchant's ship, bringing her food from afar. [15] She gets up before dawn to prepare breakfast for her household and plan the day's work for her servant girls. [16] She goes to inspect a field and buys it; with her earnings she plants a vineyard. [17] She is energetic and strong, a hard worker. [18] She makes sure her dealings are profitable; her lamp burns late into the night. [19] Her hands are busy spinning thread, her fingers twisting fiber. [20] She extends a helping hand to the poor and opens her arms to the needy. [21] She has no fear of winter for her household, for everyone has warm clothes. [22] She makes her own bedspreads. She dresses in fine linen and purple gowns. [23] Her husband is well known at the city gates, where he sits with the other civic leaders. [24] She makes belted linen garments and sashes to sell to the merchants. [25] She is clothed with strength and dignity, and she laughs without fear of the future. [26] When she speaks, her words are wise, and she gives instructions with kindness. [27] She carefully watches everything in her household and suffers nothing from laziness. [28] Her children stand and bless her. Her husband praises her: [29] "There are many virtuous and capable women in the world, but you surpass them all!" [30] Charm is deceptive, and beauty does not last; but a woman who fears the Lord will be greatly praised. [31] Reward her for all she has done. Let her deeds publicly declare her praise.

The Proverbs 31 woman is quite the lady. In verses 11, 12, 15, 17, 21 and 27, what do we learn about how she sows into her family?

_____

_____

Sometimes we can get so zealous to help other people, we forget the first people we should bless are those we are related to and those who live under our roof! Be sure to look for ways to sow money, gifts, trips, jewelry, time, words, and other special things into your own family. In what ways can you sow into your family?

1 Timothy 5:8

But those who won't care for their relatives, especially those in their own household, have denied the true faith. Such people are worse than unbelievers.

In this passage about caring for widows, what do we learn about sowing into our own families? _____

If you have aging relatives or widowed parents, you know the challenges this can bring. My mother has always been active and on the go, but in 2009, she was diagnosed with stage IV lung cancer. The doctors didn't give her much hope for a recovery. Over the next few years, God truly touched my mother and through her faith and the help of the doctors, she recovered from a deadly bout with lung cancer. Going through that battle, she never lost her wit, humor, or inner strength. However, she did lose some leg strength and eventually reached the point where she could not live independently. Her biggest fear was the idea of moving into an assisted living center. My sisters and I agonized on the best way to help our mother to be sure she had a happy and safe quality of life. We tried various living arrangements, and they all worked fine. But we never felt we had found the best option. Thankfully, our youngest sister Michelle is a saint (along with her husband, Craig), and the Lord put it in their hearts to have my mother move in with them so they could care for her. The relief and joy that was visible on my mother's face literally gave her renewed energy and made her look five years younger. While there are challenging days, the Lord has rewarded my sister and her husband with a sense of fulfillment as they honor our mom, and there is no doubt they will continue to be rewarded for the seeds they are sowing into her life.

4. Sow Offering Seeds into Those Who Teach and Preach the Word

1 Timothy 5:17-18 (NKJV)

Let the elders who rule well be counted worthy of double honor, especially those who labor in the word and doctrine. [18] For the Scripture says, "You shall not muzzle an ox while it treads out the grain," and, "The laborer *is* worthy of his wages."

What type of honor does the Lord say should be given to leaders who labor in teaching the Word and doctrine? _____

_____

How would you define double honor? _____

_____

What can we learn from the comparison between the ox and a laborer? _____

Those who labor in teaching the Word and doctrine are being compared to an ox, which must be compensated well for the work they do. Both the ox and laborers should be taken care of; they are worthy of their reward.

In your life, what spiritual leaders have taught you the Word and doctrine? _____

Have you ever honored them in a financial way? _____

_____

When you esteem the Word and recognize the value of the revelation knowledge you have received from those who teach it, you will have a heartfelt desire to return the blessing by sowing double honor.

1 Corinthians 9:7-14

[7] What soldier has to pay his own expenses? What farmer plants a vineyard and doesn't have the right to eat some of its fruit? What shepherd cares for a flock of sheep and isn't allowed to drink some of the milk? [8] Am I expressing merely a human opinion, or does the law say the same thing? [9] For the law of Moses says, "You must not muzzle an ox to keep it from eating as it treads out the grain." Was God thinking only about oxen when he said this? [10] Wasn't he actually speaking to us? Yes, it was written for us, so that the one who plows and the one who threshes the grain might both expect a share of the harvest. [11] Since we have planted spiritual seed among you, aren't we entitled to a harvest of physical food and drink? [12] If you support others who preach to you, shouldn't we have an even greater right to be supported? But we have never used this right. We would rather put up with anything than be an obstacle to the Good News about Christ. [13] Don't you realize that those who work in the temple get their meals from the offerings brought to the temple? And those who serve at the altar get a share of the sacrificial offerings. [14] In the same way, the Lord ordered that those who preach the Good News should be supported by those who benefit from it.

In light of this entire passage on the financial health of soldiers, farmers, and shepherds, what does Paul mean by "planting spiritual things" and "reaping a harvest of physical food and drink" when it comes to financial health of spiritual leaders?

_____

_____

Galatians 6:6

Those who are taught the word of God should provide for their teachers, sharing all good things with them.

What are those who are taught the Word encouraged to do for those who teach them the Word? _____

_____

Although we cannot put a price on the benefit of receiving God's Word from those He's called to minister, have you considered honoring in some type of financial or material way those individuals who have played a vital role in your spiritual growth?

5. Sow Offering Seeds into the Work of God

We've already looked at 2 Corinthians 9 and Galatians 6, which tell us a lot about sowing into the work of God (please review those passages on the previous pages!), now let's look at a few more verses.

Exodus 25:1-7

The LORD said to Moses, [2] "Tell the people of Israel to bring me their sacred offerings. Accept the contributions from all whose hearts are moved to offer them. ³ Here is a list of sacred offerings you may accept from them: gold, silver, and bronze; ⁴ blue, purple, and scarlet thread; fine linen and goat hair for cloth; ⁵ tanned ram skins and fine goatskin leather; acacia wood; ⁶ olive oil for the lamps; spices for the anointing oil and the fragrant incense; ⁷ onyx stones, and other gemstones to be set in the ephod and the priest's chest piece.

What did the Lord want the Israelites to do? _____

According to verse 2, describe the heart condition of those who gave offerings to the Lord. _____

_____

What type of offerings were they to bring? _____

What were these offerings going to be used for? _____

Exodus 35:21-29

²¹ All whose hearts were stirred and whose spirits were moved came and brought their sacred offerings to the LORD. They brought all the materials needed for the Tabernacle, for the performance of its rituals, and for the sacred garments. ²² Both men and women came, all whose hearts were willing. They brought to the LORD their offerings of gold—brooches, earrings, rings from their fingers, and necklaces. They presented gold objects of every kind as a special offering to the LORD. ²³ All those who owned the following items willingly brought them: blue, purple, and scarlet thread; fine linen and goat hair for cloth; and tanned ram skins and fine goatskin leather. ²⁴ And all who had silver and bronze objects gave them as a

sacred offering to the LORD. And those who had acacia wood brought it for use in the project.[25] All the women who were skilled in sewing and spinning prepared blue, purple, and scarlet thread, and fine linen cloth. [26] All the women who were willing used their skills to spin the goat hair into yarn. [27] The leaders brought onyx stones and the special gemstones to be set in the ephod and the priest's chestpiece. [28] They also brought spices and olive oil for the light, the anointing oil, and the fragrant incense. [29] So the people of Israel—every man and woman who was eager to help in the work the LORD had given them through Moses—brought their gifts and gave them freely to the LORD.

Who brought offerings to the Lord? _____

Describe the importance of a person's heart in giving. _____

_____

What types of things did they bring as offerings? _____

What were these offerings used for? _____

_____

Exodus 36:3-7

Moses gave them the materials donated by the people of Israel as sacred offerings for the completion of the sanctuary. But the people continued to bring additional gifts each morning. [4] Finally the craftsmen who were working on the sanctuary left their work. [5] They went to Moses and reported, "The people have given more than enough materials to complete the job the LORD has commanded us to do!" [6] So Moses gave the command, and this message was sent throughout the camp: "Men and women, don't prepare any more gifts for the sanctuary. We have enough!" So the people stopped bringing their sacred offerings. [7] Their contributions were more than enough to complete the whole project.

This passage is every pastor's dream! I don't know of a single pastor who has ever told his or her congregation to stop bringing offerings to church! Let's look at this amazing account.

What did Moses give to those who were building the sanctuary?

_____

What did the people do continually? _____

In verses 4-5, what did the builders tell Moses? _____

_____

In verse 6, what did Moses tell all of God's people? _____

_____

In verse 7, what happened as a result of the generous giving of offerings? _____

John 6:5-13

Jesus soon saw a huge crowd of people coming to look for him. Turning to Philip, he asked, "Where can we buy bread to feed all these people?" [6] He was testing Philip, for he already knew what he was going to do. [7] Philip replied, "Even if we worked for months, we wouldn't have enough money to feed them!" [8] Then Andrew, Simon Peter's brother, spoke up. [9] "There's a young boy here with five barley loaves and two fish. But what good is that with this huge crowd?" [10] "Tell everyone to sit down," Jesus said.

So they all sat down on the grassy slopes. (The men alone numbered about 5,000.) [11] Then Jesus took the loaves, gave thanks to God, and distributed them to the people. Afterward he did the same with the fish. And they all ate as much as they wanted. [12] After everyone was full, Jesus told his disciples, "Now gather the leftovers, so that nothing is wasted." [13] So they picked up the pieces and filled twelve baskets with scraps left by the people who had eaten from the five barley loaves.

This is the story of a little boy who gave an offering to Jesus. It shows that Jesus can do miraculous things with our offerings!

According to verse 9, what did the little lad have to offer to Jesus?

_____

What did Jesus do with that offering of five barley loaves and two fish? _____

How many people (including the men and an estimated number of women and children) did Jesus feed to the full with the five loaves and two small fish? _____

_____

According to verses 12 and 13, how many baskets did they fill with the scraps left by the people who had eaten their fill?

_____

Although the Bible doesn't tell us directly, who do you think went home with those 12 baskets of bread and fish?

_____

God can do miracles when we give Him offerings!

Luke 5:1-7 (NKJV)

So it was, as the multitude pressed about Him to hear the word of God, that He stood by the Lake of Gennesaret, [2] and saw two boats standing by the lake; but the fishermen had gone from them and were washing *their* nets. [3] Then He got into one of the boats, which was Simon's, and asked him to put out a little from the land. And He sat down and taught the multitudes from the boat. [4] When He had stopped speaking, He said to Simon, "Launch out into the deep and let down your nets for a catch." [5] But Simon answered and said to Him, "Master, we have toiled all night and caught nothing; nevertheless at Your word I will let down the net." [6] And when they had done this, they caught a great number of fish, and their net was breaking. [7] So they signaled to *their* partners in the other boat to come and help them. And they came and filled both the boats, so that they began to sink.

This is the well-known story of Peter's net-breaking, boat-sinking catch of fish! Jesus had a need. Peter had a seed. Peter sowed the seed of his boat into the need Jesus had to preach the Word and Peter ended up reaping a net-breaking, boat-sinking harvest of fish!

In verse 1, what did the multitude want from Jesus? _____

In verse 3, whose boat did Jesus need? _____

What did Jesus ask Peter (Simon) to do? _____

In verse 3, what did Jesus do with the gift of Peter's boat? _____

_____

In verse 4, what did Jesus tell Peter? _____

In verse 5, Peter was tired and reluctant, but what was it that convinced Peter? _____

In verse 6-7, what type of harvest did Peter reap on the seed of sowing his boat into Jesus' ministry? _____

What seed is God asking you to sow into a need He would like to see fulfilled? _____

Luke 6:31-38

[31] Do to others as you would like them to do to you. [32] If you love only those who love you, why should you get credit for that? Even sinners love those who love them! [33] And if you do good only to those who do good to you, why should you get credit? Even sinners do that much! [34] And if you lend money only to those who can repay you, why should you get credit? Even sinners will lend to other sinners for a full return. [35] Love your enemies! Do good to them. Lend to them without expecting to be repaid. Then your reward from heaven will be very great, and you will truly be acting as children of the Most High, for he is kind to those who are unthankful and wicked. [36] You must be compassionate, just as your Father is compassionate. [37] Do not judge others, and you will not be judged. Do not condemn others, or it will all come back against you. Forgive others, and you will be forgiven. [38] Give, and you will receive. Your gift will return to you in full—pressed down, shaken together to make room for more, running over, and poured into your lap. The amount you give will determine the amount you get back.

According to verse 31, what should we do to others? _____

In verses 32-37, list the types of things we should give to others.

_____

In verses 34-35, what does the Lord tell us to do with our money?

_____

According to verse 38, if we give, what will happen? _____

_____

In what way will our gift return? _____

_____

What role does the amount we give play in determining the amount we get back? _____

When it comes to sowing, we always reap more than we sow after we sow and in proportion to the amount we have sown. We always reap the measure we sowed multiplied.

Litmus Test Alert: It's great to know that when we give to others, it will return to us in full and according to the amount we give out. But here's the surprising litmus test. If people aren't giving to us in any measure, we need to contact Houston, because we have a problem. When good things like love, compassion, forgiveness, and finances are not coming back to us, it's a sign that we are not giving them to others.

We can't expect truckloads being given to us, if we only give to others in teaspoons. According to this passage, we receive multiplied measures of what we give to others. If we sow teaspoons full of love, money, or compassion, we will reap multiplied teaspoons full of love, money, and compassion.

For example, maybe you need to start by giving to others in the $10 amount. If you do, you will reap multiplied $10 amounts. Then, eventually you'll be able to bump up your giving to the $50 amount, and you'll reap multiplied $50 measures. Eventually you'll be able to give in $100 amounts and then $1000 amounts and $20,000 amounts, and if you stay with it, maybe even $1 million dollar amounts. At each level, you will reap the multiplied version of that amount.

We saw this principle at work in the early days of sowing financial seeds. During a particular season in our lives, we noticed that we were receiving an unusual number of random $50 gift cards to restaurants and stores. As we thought about it, we realized that we were receiving back the multiplied measure of what we had been sowing! For the prior season, we had determined we were going to do most of our sowing for offerings and gifts in $50 increments. That was our standard measure, and when we realized that we had reaped a multiplied amount of $50 gift cards, we decided to move the decimal! We decided to make $100 our standard giving increment for offerings and gifts over and above our tithe, and wouldn't you know, we started to receive multiplied blessings and gifts in the $100 amount. Dewey's got nothing on God's Decimal System! Wherever we place the decimal, we will reap in that measure.

What can we learn from this? If you are not seeing big harvests in your life, it's very possible you are not giving in a big enough measure. (Ouch, I know! That is one big knuckle sandwich and wake up call, isn't it? So, if you want the zeros on the end of what you receive to get larger, you'll have to start sowing seed with more zeroes on the end. Don't get mad. Get glad! God's trying to help get more to you and through you! That is all. At ease.)

Philippians 4:15-20 (MSG)

15-17 You Philippians well know, and you can be sure I'll never forget it, that when I first left Macedonia province, venturing out with the Message, not one church helped out in the give-and-take of this work except you. You were the only one. Even while I was in Thessalonica, you helped out—and not only once, but twice. Not that I'm looking for handouts, but I do want you to experience the blessing that issues from generosity.[18-20] And now I have it all—and keep getting more! The gifts you sent with Epaphroditus were more than enough, like a sweet-smelling sacrifice roasting on the altar, filling the air with fragrance, pleasing God no end. You can be sure that God will take care of everything you need, his generosity exceeding even yours in the glory that pours from Jesus. Our God and Father abounds in glory that just pours out into eternity. Yes.

What did the Philippian church do to help the Apostle Paul with preaching the gospel message? _____

_____

How often did they contribute to his ministry? _____

_____

What did Paul say he wanted them to experience for their generosity?

_____

In what way would God reward the Philippians for their generosity?

_____

As you can see, not only can we sow as individuals, but many businesses and churches have made giving a part of their protocol. We know a church in Alaska that makes it a priority to host a missions conference every year where they bring over twenty missionaries back from the mission field to sow rest, encouragement, and financial blessings into their lives and ministries. A few years ago, they were able to raise almost $1 million dollars from their congregation to sow into missionaries' lives. They are sowing good seed into good ground, both temporally and eternally!

Did you know you have a heavenly debit and credit account? Look at the way the Amplified Bible puts this same passage.

Philippians 4:15-19 (AMPC)

[15] And you Philippians yourselves well know that in the early days of the Gospel ministry, when I left Macedonia, no church (assembly) entered into partnership with me and opened up [a debit and credit] account in giving and receiving except you only. [16] For even in Thessalonica you sent [me contributions] for my needs, not only once but a second time. [17] Not that I seek or am eager for [your] gift, but I do seek and am eager for the fruit which increases to your credit [the harvest of blessing that is accumulating to your account]. [18] But I have [your full payment] and more; I have everything I need and am amply supplied, now that I have received from Epaphroditus the gifts you sent me. [They are the] fragrant odor of an offering and sacrifice which God welcomes and in which He delights. [19] And my God will liberally supply (fill to the full) your every need according to His riches in glory in Christ Jesus.

6. Sow Offering Seeds into the Future

We have the opportunity to invest our lives and our wealth into things that will last for eternity. If we will take some time to intentionally plan for the present and the future, our finances can be used to influence this world for Christ long after we leave the earth to go be with the Lord. Let's close out this session by giving some thought to sowing seeds into the future.

Proverbs 24:3-4 (TLB)

Any enterprise is built by wise planning, becomes strong through common sense, and profits wonderfully by keeping abreast of the facts.

What three things cause an enterprise to be built? _____

_____

Have you given any time to building your legacy by planning your giving wisely? _____

_____

Have you been strengthening the influence of your life by giving with common sense? _____

Have you determined to see your life profit by investing your finances in churches, ministries, and gospel preaching organizations with a healthy track record? _____

Proverbs 14:8 (TLB)

The wise man looks ahead. The fool attempts to fool himself and won't face facts.

What does a wise man do? _____

There is something wise about looking ahead towards eternity to be sure you have lived a life that is rich towards God.

Proverbs 10:7 (NKJV)

The memory of the righteous is blessed, but the name of the wicked will rot.

What happens to the memory (legacy) of the righteous? _____

_____

1 Corinthians 3:10-15 (NKJV)

[10]According to the grace of God which was given to me, as a wise master builder I have laid the foundation, and another builds on it. But let each one take heed how he builds on it. [11] For no other foundation can anyone lay than that which is laid, which is Jesus Christ. [12] Now if anyone builds on this foundation *with* gold, silver, precious stones, wood, hay, straw, [13] each one's work will become clear; for the Day will declare it, because it will be revealed by fire; and the fire will test each one's work, of what sort it is. [14] If anyone's work which he has built on *it* endures, he will receive a reward. [15] If anyone's work is burned, he will suffer loss; but he himself will be saved, yet so as through fire.

As Christians, we are encouraged to build on the foundation of Jesus Christ in our lives with eternal materials that will stand the test of fire. Generally, this means that we should build our lives with an eye towards eternal things. In literal terms, it's interesting that the Apostle Paul used monetary items like gold, silver, and precious stones to describe the way believers can build a lasting, eternal legacy that God will reward.

What types of things can we use to build on the foundation of Jesus Christ? _____

What materials will endure the test of fire? _____

What does this passage teach us about using our material wealth for eternal kingdom purposes? _____

Matthew 6:19-21 (NKJV)

"Do not lay up for yourselves treasures on earth, where moth and rust destroy and where thieves break in and steal; [20] but lay up for yourselves treasures in heaven, where neither moth nor rust destroys and where thieves do not break in and steal. [21] For where your treasure is, there your heart will be also.

Who can we lay up treasures for? _____

What happens to the treasures we lay up for ourselves on earth?

_____

What happens to the treasures we lay up for ourselves in heaven?

_____

How do we lay up treasures in heaven? _____

_____

The Bible has a lot to say about laying up treasures and the rewards and crowns awaiting believers. We can lay up treasures by loving Jesus, giving a cold cup of water to one of His disciples, facing persecution, sowing into His kingdom, using our gifts in serving the Lord, and in many other ways. When we seek first the kingdom of God and His righteousness, all kinds of things are added to us in this life and the life to come.

Where is our heart? _____

When do you think we can access the treasures we lay up in heaven?

_____

Notice, Jesus said we are laying up treasures "for ourselves." That's an interesting thought, isn't it? Often, we think of accessing those treasures once we get to heaven, and that is true. God has a lot in store for us in heaven! All kinds of treasures await us. According to 1 Corinthians 2:9 (NKJV), ". . . it is written: 'Eye has not seen, nor ear heard, nor have entered into the heart of man the things which God has prepared for those who love Him.'" Exciting things await us!

But, I wonder if there is more to the idea of laying up treasures in heaven than we realize. Perhaps God wants us to understand that we can access those treasures in this life, too. If we are storing up treasures for ourselves in heaven, will we need them in heaven? Heaven's streets are paved with gold and Jesus is building mansions for us, so what kinds of treasures will we need there? Perhaps the real need for these treasures is here while we are on earth. In other words, when we "lay up for ourselves treasures in heaven" through giving God our wealth, time, and talents, perhaps it is so we can make a withdrawal while we are still here. Do you see that? Friends, I encourage you to be intentional about storing up for yourself treasures in heaven, and when you need to make withdrawals, just ask the Lord.

Did this session excite you? I hope so. Let's wrap up by answering a few more common questions.

COMMON QUESTIONS AND ANSWERS

1. We shouldn't give to get, should we?

You may have heard someone say something like, "We shouldn't give to get" or "We should just give because we love God, with no desire or expectation to receive anything back." It sounds good, doesn't it? There is a truth in those statements. Even if the Lord didn't promise any type of harvest or rewards for our faith-filled giving, we should still give to the Lord out of a heart of love. But there is nothing wrong with believing God's Word and His promises to those who sow generously. Can you imagine how strange it would be for a farmer to sow seeds into hundreds of acres and then say, "I am not sowing seed to get a harvest. I just love God, and I like to sow seed with no expectations." You might wonder about that farmer!

Farmers sow fields with seed expecting to grow crops and reap a harvest! We should do the same. There is nothing wrong with giving to get or better put, sowing to reap.

2. Isn't this idea of sowing and reaping just a carnal get-rich-quick scheme?

God wants His people to get wealth and to be generous, and as we cooperate with His Word, we can live in the flow of God's economy.

The idea of a get-rich-quick scheme is the exact opposite of what the Bible teaches. Unfortunately, human nature likes to look for the short cuts. Let's see what God's Word says about recognizing a get-rich-quick scheme.

Proverbs 13:11 (NKJV)

Wealth gained by dishonesty will be diminished, but he who gathers by labor will increase.

The Amplified Bible Classic Edition makes this verse a little clearer. It reads like this:

Wealth [not earned but] won in haste *or* unjustly *or* from the production of things for vain or detrimental use [such as riches] will dwindle away, but he who gathers little by little will increase [his riches].

Proverbs 20:21 (NKJV)

An inheritance gained hastily at the beginning will not be blessed at the end.

Proverbs 28:20, 22

The trustworthy person will get a rich reward, but a person who wants quick riches will get into trouble . . . [22] Greedy people try to get rich quick but don't realize they're headed for poverty.

What do you learn from these verses of Scripture?_____

_____

_____

3. Won't too much money tempt me to fall away from the Lord?

This is possible, but it depends upon what type of heart you have. Having too much money probably wouldn't tempt you to fall away from the Lord any more than not having enough money would. It's a matter of your heart being in the right place. By making money your idol, you could fall away from the Lord. But that's true about anything we might put in place of God. Hopefully as a believer, you have developed a strong relationship with the Lord so that His prospering you would only cause you to give thanks and praise to Him for His abundant blessings and motivate you to be even more generous towards gospel efforts around the world.

Let's look at this question in light of human relationships. Would too much money cause you to fall away from your spouse or close friend? It all depends on where your heart is. The thing that could cause us to fall away from the Lord is a cold heart, not cold hard cash.

When our affection, trust, and faith is in the Lord, the blessings God brings into our lives aren't the cake; they are just the icing on the cake, and we are free to be generous.

Acts 20:32-35 is a great passage to wrap up our study: "And now I entrust you to God and the message of his grace that is able to build you up and give you an inheritance with all those he has set apart for himself. I have never coveted anyone's silver or gold or fine clothes. You know that these hands of mine have worked to supply my own needs and even the needs of those who were with me. And I have been a constant example of how you can help those in need by working hard. You should remember the words of the Lord Jesus: 'It is more blessed to give than to receive.'"

4. Isn't God sovereign when it comes to prospering people?

Does God sovereignly choose to prosper certain people? Does God in His sovereignty only allow "those He can trust" to be blessed with wealth? Does the Bible teach us that God has the prerogative to prosper some people while keeping others in humbler means?

From what we've studied, I trust you can see that when it comes to wealth and prosperity, God gives all of us a choice. Everyone, regardless of gender, race, class, or nationality, can move up economically as we trust the Lord, believe His Word, and employ His principles of generosity.

2 Thessalonians 3:10-12 (NKJV)

For even when we were with you, we commanded you this: If anyone will not work, neither shall he eat. [11] For we hear that there are some who walk among you in a disorderly manner, not working at all, but are busybodies. [12] Now those who are such we command and exhort through our Lord Jesus Christ that they work in quietness and eat their own bread.

If a person is able but unwilling to work, what should be the result?

_____

Describe a busybody or disorderly person. _____

_____

What does the Lord want these people to do? _____

_____

Joshua 1:8 (NKJV)

This Book of the Law shall not depart from your mouth, but you shall meditate in it day and night, that you may observe to do according to all that is written in it. For then you will make your way prosperous, and then you will have good success.

When we make living by God's Word our goal, according to this verse, who makes our way prosperous and successful? _____

_____

Deuteronomy 30:15-20

[15] Now listen! Today I am giving you a choice between life and death, between prosperity and disaster. [16] For I command you this day to love the LORD your God and to keep his commands, decrees, and regulations by walking in his ways. If you do this, you will live and multiply, and the LORD your God will bless you and the land you are about to enter and occupy.[17] But if your heart turns away and you refuse to listen, and if you are drawn away to serve and worship other gods, [18] then I warn you now that you will certainly be destroyed. You will not live a long, good life in the land you are crossing the Jordan to occupy.[19] Today I have given you the choice between life and death, between blessings and curses. Now I call on heaven and earth to witness the choice you make. Oh, that you would choose life, so that you and your descendants might live! [20] You can make this choice by loving the LORD your God, obeying him, and committing yourself firmly to him. This is the key to your life. And if you love and obey the LORD, you will live long in the land the LORD swore to give your ancestors Abraham, Isaac, and Jacob.

While we are not under the law any longer, there is a moral principle of loving God, living in a way that pleases Him, and experiencing a blessed life. You will notice that throughout the Word of God, while He is the Sovereign Lord, in most matters, God gives us the opportunity to choose.

According to verses 15 and 19, whose choice is it to walk in life, prosperity, and blessings? _____

_____

LET'S GET PRACTICAL

I hope through this session, you've been encouraged and challenged to seek the Lord as you sow offering seeds in a generous way. Here are a few practical ways to put this into practice:

1) In addition to your tithe, decide on the amount of seed you want to sow for the next month or six months or year. I encourage you to put it into your budget. Is it $10 at a time? One hundred dollars a month? Five thousand per year? You also might want to consider any extra income, unexpected income, or gifts as seed to sow.

2) Think about the material possessions you have or the other sharable advantages or blessings you could sow into others. Make a list of things you would like to give away to stir up the spirit of generosity and to devise generous things.

3) Listen to the promptings of the Holy Spirit and identify any individuals or ministries that are on your heart, and begin devising a generous plan to bless them.

4) Start giving! As you experience the joy of cheerful giving and faith-filled sowing, may you truly experience the truth of these words from Acts 20:35, "It is more blessed to give than to receive!"

JOURNAL ENTRY

To get the most out of this chapter, take a few moments to journal your thoughts and/or prayers.

_____

_____

_____

_____

_____

_____

_____

_____

_____

_____

_____

_____

_____

_____

SESSION 4:
THE INVESTMENT OF ALMS

———— ✦ ————

O kay, have you ever considered the option of giving God a loan? Seriously. Loaning to the One who owns all the silver and gold and the cattle on a thousand hills? Well, that's exactly what Proverbs 19:17 says, "If you help the poor, you are lending to the LORD—and he will repay you!"

It seems there has been an incredible uptick in the number of Christians interested and passionate about feeding the poor, digging water wells for those in poverty, rescuing victims of sex trafficking, building homes for widows and orphans, microfinancing single moms in third world countries, and seeing justice served for the underprivileged. It's phenomenal to hear about and be a part of the work so many people, agencies, and ministries are doing in large cities, inner cities, slums, brothels, remote villages, and some of the darkest and poorest places on earth.

A friend of ours decided to use his 40th birthday as an occasion to help the poor. Instead of receiving gifts for his birthday, he asked his friends to consider making a donation to a ministry that digs wells for those in third world countries.

The Bible tells us God takes it personally when we help the poor. Jesus spent much of His ministry doing the very same thing, going throughout all kinds of villages teaching the truths about God, preaching the Gospel, and healing the sick and less fortunate.

You've likely heard the saying, "Give a man a fish and feed him for a day; teach a man to fish and feed him for a lifetime." Both are needed. We "give a man a fish" by using our wealth to help the less fortunate. We "teach a man to fish," when we empower him with education, marketable skills, and experience so he has a fighting chance to succeed for the rest of life his life. But, we shouldn't stop there. We should "teach a man to give a fish" so he can respond to the Lord's generosity and enter into the flow of God's economy too!

Let's look at what Jesus said about bringing good news to the poor.

Luke 4:18

The Spirit of the LORD is upon me, for he has anointed me to bring Good News to the poor. He has sent me to proclaim that captives will be released, that the blind will see, that the oppressed will be set free.

What did Jesus say He was anointed to do? _____

What would good news to the spiritually poor sound like? _____

_____

What would good news to the relationally poor sound like? _____

_____

What would good news to the physically or financially poor sound like? _____

LOVE IS THE GOAL

Love is the heart behind all we do.

Have you noticed some people are motivated by mercy and are really good at giving care, being compassionate, and oozing God's sweet love to everyone they meet? This is such a wonderful gift.

Others, not so much.

In a world of tremendous need, whether you are mercy motivated or in the "not so much" category, it's easy, in an effort to survive, to put our emotions in neutral or on autopilot and help people robotically. When we do that, we lose the joy God wants us to experience as we help others.

All of us have to guard against becoming desensitized and detached from the people we serve. This is especially challenging for those who serve in law enforcement, medicine, social services, mental health, ministry, or a host of other occupations where you are constantly in the "giving out" mode. The needs around us can be overwhelming, and none of us are equipped to carry every burden. When we try to help everyone, we run the risk of developing the Messiah complex and burning out. (Thankfully, there is only one Messiah, Jesus. So the next time you feel responsible for feeding, rescuing, and healing the entire world, just repeat this several times, "I am not the Messiah. I am not the Messiah.")

I understand the challenge. Learning how to remain empathetic and compassionate while maintaining a healthy detachment from those we are serving can be tough. We tend to tilt. We either get too vested and foster codependent relationships, or we get so detached, we become numb zombies. Both are bad. I know that I have been through seasons where I've felt depleted of all mercy and compassion and I needed the Lord to rejuvenate His indwelling love. Spending some alone time with the Lord to get His perspective, to read His Word, to pray, sing, and worship Him is the best way I have found to refresh and soften my own heart so His love can flow freely. When I remind myself that I am His conduit (not the source of power or supply), I find His mercy flows through me more freely, and I feel His heart of compassion for people revived.

Do you need the Lord to reset His love in your inner man? Let's look at the Scriptures.

Romans 5:5

For we know how dearly God loves us, because he has given us the Holy Spirit to fill our hearts with his love.

Who loves us dearly? _____

What has the Holy Spirit filled our hearts with? _____

We don't have to manufacture love. We just have to yield to the love He has already put in our hearts and let it flow out generously to those around us.

1 Corinthians 13:3

If I gave everything I have to the poor and even sacrificed my body, I could boast about it; but if I didn't love others, I would have gained nothing.

If you give everything to the poor but don't love others, what do you gain? _____

You might want to reread 1 Corinthians 13:4-8 to be reminded of God's definition for love.

1 Timothy 1:5 (NIV)

The goal of this command is love, which comes from a pure heart and a good conscience and a sincere faith.

What is the goal of God's command? _____

This comes from a _____ heart, and a _____ conscience and a _____ faith.

Mark 12:28-31

One of the teachers of religious law was standing there listening to the debate. He realized that Jesus had answered well, so he asked, "Of all the commandments, which is the most import- ant?" [29] Jesus replied, "The most important commandment is this: 'Listen, O Israel! The LORD our God is the one and only LORD. [30] And you must love the Lord your God with all your heart, all your soul, all your mind, and all your strength.' [31] The second is equally important: 'Love your neighbor as yourself.' No other commandment is greater than these."

What is the most important commandment? _____

_____

What is the second most important commandment? _____

_____

How does this play out in your life? _____

_____

2 Corinthians 8:1-24

Now I want you to know, dear brothers and sisters, what God in his kindness has done through the churches in Macedonia. [2] They are being tested by many troubles, and they are very poor. But they are also filled with abundant joy, which has overflowed in rich generosity. [3] For I can testify that they gave not only what they could afford, but far more. And they did it of their own free will. [4] They begged us again and again for the privilege of sharing in the gift for the believers in Jerusalem. [5] They even did more than we had hoped, for their first action was to give themselves to the Lord and to us, just as God wanted them to do. [6] So we have urged Titus, who encouraged your giving in the first place, to return to you and encourage you to finish this ministry of giving. [7] Since you excel in so many ways—in your faith, your gifted speakers, your knowledge, your enthusiasm, and your love from us—I want you to excel also in this gracious act of giving. [8] I am not commanding you to do this. But I am testing how genuine your love is by comparing it with the eagerness of the other churches. [9] You know the generous grace of our Lord Jesus Christ. Though he was rich, yet for your sakes he became poor, so that by his poverty he could make you rich. [10] Here is my advice: It would be good for you to finish what you started a year ago. Last year you were the first who wanted to give, and you were the first to begin doing it. [11] Now you should finish what you started. Let the eagerness you showed in the beginning be matched now by your giving. Give in proportion to what you have. [12] Whatever you give is acceptable if you give it eagerly. And give according to what you have, not what you don't have. [13] Of course, I don't mean your giving should make life easy for others and hard for yourselves. I only mean that there should be some equality. [14] Right now you have plenty and can help those who are in need. Later, they will have plenty and can share with you when you need it. In this way, things will be equal. [15] As the Scriptures say, "Those who gathered a lot had nothing left over, and those who gathered only a little had enough." [16] But thank God! He has given Titus the same enthusiasm for you that I have. [17] Titus welcomed our request that he visit you again. In fact, he himself was very eager to go and see you. [18] We are also sending another brother with Titus. All the churches praise him as a preacher of the Good News. [19] He was appointed by the churches to accompany us as we take the offering to Jerusalem—a service that glorifies the Lord and shows our eagerness to help. [20] We are traveling together to guard against any criticism for the way we are handling this generous gift. [21] We are careful to be honorable before the Lord, but we also want everyone else to see that we are honorable. [22] We are also sending with them another of our brothers who has proven himself many times and has shown on many occasions how eager he is. He is now even more enthusiastic because of his great confidence in you. [23] If anyone asks about Titus, say that he is my partner who works with me to help you. And the brothers with him have been sent by the churches, and they bring honor to Christ. [24] So show them your love, and prove to all the churches that our boasting about you is justified.

This long passage is worth reading. Every verse is loaded with talk about the generous giving of believers to the poor and needy. It's all summarized in verse 24.

What does giving to the poor show?_____

How does giving demonstrate our love? _____

Do you get the idea? Love is the goal.

GOD NOTICES THOSE WHO GIVE TO THE POOR

Matthew 6:1-4 (KJV)

Take heed that ye do not your alms before men, to be seen of them: otherwise ye have no reward of your Father which is in heaven. [2] Therefore when thou doest thine alms, do not sound a trumpet before thee, as the hypocrites do in the synagogues and in the streets, that they may have glory of men. Verily I say unto you, They have their reward. [3] But when thou doest alms, let not thy left hand know what thy right hand doeth: [4] That thine alms may be in secret: and thy Father which seeth in secret himself shall reward thee openly.

Alms: The Greek word translated "alms" is *eleemosune*.[1] Its meaning includes compassion exercised towards the poor, beneficence.

How are we *not to* give our gifts (alms) to the poor?_____

_____

How are we *to* give our gifts (alms) to the poor? _____

_____

How will God reward us? _____

Why do you think it's important to keep your giving to the poor confidential and secret? _____

Proverbs 19:17

If you help the poor, you are lending to the LORD—and he will repay you!

What a powerful verse!

If you help the poor, what are you doing?_____

_____

What will the Lord do for you when you help the poor? _____

_____

Do you think God makes good on paying back His loans? _____

_____

Deuteronomy 15:7-11

But if there are any poor Israelites in your towns when you arrive in the land the LORD your God is giving you, do not be hard-hearted or tightfisted toward them. ⁸ Instead, be generous and lend them whatever they need. ⁹ Do not be mean-spirited and refuse someone a loan because the year for canceling debts is close at hand. If you refuse to make the loan and the needy person cries out to the LORD, you will be considered guilty of sin. ¹⁰ Give generously to the poor, not grudgingly, for the LORD your God will bless you in everything you do. ¹¹ There will always be some in the land who are poor. That is why I am commanding you to share freely with the poor and with other Israelites in need.

According to verses 7 through 9, what type of attitude are we to have toward the poor? _____

According to verse 10, how are we to treat the poor? _____

_____

What does the Lord promise to those who help the needy? _____

_____

Psalm 41:1

Oh, the joys of those who are kind to the poor! The Lord rescues them when they are in trouble.

How should we treat the poor? _____

What do those who are kind to the poor get to experience? _____

_____

Proverbs 22:9

Blessed are those who are generous, because they feed the poor.

Years ago, we visited our friends Pastor Joe and Barbara Sorce from New beginnings Christian Church in Brick, New Jersey and observed their incredible outreach to feed the needy in their area. Then we visited our friends, Pastors Bill and Sandy Scheer from Guts Church in Tulsa, Oklahoma, where we saw their Friday Groceries Ministries, a very effective outreach that feeds the poor. We were inspired to develop and launch our own version of Friday Groceries to feed Southwest Michigan. Since then, we've established Mobile Groceries to take bags of food into various counties throughout Southwest Michigan. The no-strings-attached approach to loving people with bags of groceries has given those in need a real sense of dignity as they receive bags of healthy foods to feed their families. Not only are the less fortunate being cared for, but we have been elated to see the joy and blessings that have come into the lives of those who volunteer to pick, pack, pray, serve, love, load and hug those in need week after week. Just as Proverbs 22:9 says, those who feed the poor are truly blessed!

What should we do for the poor?_____

A person who is generous and gives to the poor shall be what?

_____

Proverbs 28:27

Whoever gives to the poor will lack nothing, but those who close their eyes to poverty will be cursed.

Whoever gives to the poor will lack what? _____

What happens if we close our eyes to the poor? _____

_____

Acts 10:1-4

In Caesarea there lived a Roman army officer named Cornelius, who was a captain of the Italian Regiment. [2] He was a devout, God-fearing man, as was everyone in his household. He gave generously to the poor and prayed regularly to God. [3] One afternoon about three o'clock, he had a vision in which he saw an angel of God coming toward him. "Cornelius!" the angel said. [4] Cornelius stared at him in terror. "What is it, sir?" he asked the angel. And the angel replied, "Your prayers and gifts to the poor have been received by God as an offering!"

In Acts 10 and 11, we get the whole story of this Roman army officer and his family. The Lord used Peter to bring the message of salvation through Jesus Christ and the power of the Holy Spirit to his entire household. What can we learn from this story about Cornelius and his love for the poor?

Describe Cornelius, according to verse 2. _____

_____

According to verse 4, what had been received by God?

_____

Obviously, God heard Cornelius's prayers and saw his giving to the poor. As a result, Cornelius and his household were the first Gentile converts after the resurrection of Jesus Christ. Do you see the interesting connection? He gave to the poor, lending to the Lord, and the Lord certainly repaid him and his whole household!

HOW CAN WE HELP AND EMPOWER THE POOR?

Romans 12:9-13

Don't just pretend to love others. Really love them. Hate what is wrong. Hold tightly to what is good. [10] Love each other with genuine affection, and take delight in honoring each other.

[11] Never be lazy, but work hard and serve the Lord enthusiastically. [12] Rejoice in our confident hope. Be patient in trouble, and keep on praying. [13] When God's people are in need, be ready to help them. Always be eager to practice hospitality.

According to verses 9 and 10, how are we to love others? _____

_____

Describe this type of love. _____

_____

According to verse 13, in what ways are we to help God's people in need? _____

1 John 3:17-19

If someone has enough money to live well and sees a brother or sister in need but shows no compassion—how can God's love be in that person? [18] Dear children, let's not merely say that we love each other; let us show the truth by our actions. [19] Our actions will show that we belong to the truth, so we will be confident when we stand before God.

If a Christian has enough money to live well, what should they do?

_____

Our love is shown by what? _____

What are some ways you can empower those who are less fortunate in your sphere of influence? _____

_____

Proverbs 31:20

She extends a helping hand to the poor and opens her arms to the needy.

What does a good woman do? _____

In what ways can you help to empower the poor and needy? _____

_____

Matthew 25:34-40

Then the King will say to those on his right, "Come, you who are blessed by my Father, inherit the Kingdom prepared for you from the creation of the world. [35] For I was hungry, and you fed me. I was thirsty, and you gave me a drink. I was a stranger, and you invited me into your home. [36] I was naked, and you gave me clothing. I was sick, and you cared for me. I was in prison, and you visited me." [37] Then these righteous ones will reply, "Lord, when did we ever see you hungry and feed you? Or thirsty and give you something to drink? [38] Or a stranger and show you hospitality? Or naked and give you clothing? [39] When did we ever see you sick or in prison and visit you?" [40] And the King will say, "I tell you the truth, when you did it to one of the least of these my brothers and sisters, you were doing it to me!"

Many Bible scholars believe this passage is a reference to the judgment of nations that were helpful to or harmful towards Israel. From this passage, we can also learn principles on caring for those in need.

What are we supposed to do for the following people:

The hungry? _____

The thirsty? _____

Strangers? _____

The naked? _____

The sick? _____

Those in prison? _____

Has the Lord put any of these things on your heart? _____

If so, describe what you've been sensing._____

COMMON QUESTIONS

1. Didn't Jesus say the poor will always be with us?

Yes, Jesus did say this, but what was He talking about? Did He mean to infer that since we will always have the poor with us, we shouldn't help them? Or did He mean that we should not prosper?

This doesn't make any logical sense. Of course God wants us to help the poor, and He wants us to prosper. How can we help the poor unless we have wealth?

In other words, just because there will always be people who drop out of school before they graduate, doesn't mean we should drop out and not graduate. We should graduate and then help those who are struggling to finish school. Just because other people don't fulfill their potential, doesn't mean we should not fulfill ours. We should fulfill our potential and help those who need a boost to fulfill theirs.

Let's look at this passage of Scripture in John.

John 12:1-8

Six days before the Passover celebration began, Jesus arrived in Bethany, the home of Lazarus—the man he had raised from the dead. ²A dinner was prepared in Jesus' honor. Martha served, and Lazarus was among those who ate with him. ³Then Mary took a twelve-ounce jar of expensive perfume made from essence of nard, and she anointed Jesus' feet with it, wiping his feet with her hair. The house was filled with the fragrance. ⁴But Judas Iscariot, the disciple who would soon betray him, said, ⁵"That perfume was worth a year's wages. It should have been sold and the money given to the poor." ⁶Not that he cared for the poor—he was a thief, and since he was in charge of the disciples' money, he often stole some for himself. ⁷Jesus replied, "Leave her alone. She did this in preparation for my burial. ⁸You will always have the poor among you, but you will not always have me."

When Jesus said, "You will always have the poor among you," He was merely stating a fact of life. It would be similar to us saying, "You will always have the sick among you" or "You will always have unbelievers among you." These are true statements, but they don't mean that we should aspire to be poor. Instead, we should do our part to resolve the plight of those in need.

There are a few other interesting things to note from this passage.

First, Jesus seems to be making a distinction between Himself and the poor. He could have identified with the poor by saying, "You will always have *us* poor among you," but Jesus contrasted Himself with the poor when He said, "You will always have the poor among you, but you will not always have me." Jesus knew there would always be poor people among us, so He brought good news to the poor. (See the next Common Question for more on this topic.)

Second, Judas didn't care about the poor; he was a thief. Interestingly, he was the most vocal person when it came to the way the disciples' funds should be used. Sadly, Judas-types are still alive and well in some churches. These Judases don't give a dollar to the church, and they don't care about the gospel mission of the church or about helping the poor, but they are often the most vocal in their opinions on where the money should be spent. #truthbomb

2. Wasn't Jesus poor?

In 2 Corinthians 8:9 (NKJV), it says, "For you know the grace of our Lord Jesus Christ, that though He was rich, yet for your sakes He became poor, that you through His poverty might become rich." At first glance, you could almost get the idea that Jesus lived as a poor man. However, when we consider the rest of the Scriptures, we learn a few things that indicate quite the opposite.

Compared to the wealth and riches of heaven, when Jesus left heaven and came to earth it could be considered "becoming poor." But His earthly standard of living did not appear to be poor for these reasons:

1) His parents received quite a treasure trove of gold, frankincense, and myrrh from the wise men at His birth (Matthew 2:11).

2) He had numerous financial partners for His ministry (Luke 8:3).

3) He had enough money to require a treasurer and enough money that when this treasurer embezzled from the stash, no one noticed (John 12:6).

4) He traveled on a donkey colt, considered to be the vehicle of transportation for royalty (Matthew 21:4-7).

5) His clothing was expensive enough that the soldiers at the cross drew lots to see who got it (Matthew 27:35).

3. Doesn't the Bible tell us to desire neither poverty nor riches?

Not necessarily.

Proverbs 30:1-9

The sayings of Agur son of Jakeh contain this message. I am weary, O God; I am weary and worn out, O God. [2] I am too stupid to be human, and I lack common sense. [3] I have not mastered human wisdom, nor do I know the Holy One. [4] Who but God goes up to heaven and comes back down? Who holds the wind in his fists? Who wraps up the oceans in his cloak? Who has created the whole wide world? What is his name—and his son's name? Tell me if you know! [5] Every word of God proves true. He is a shield to all who come to him for protection. [6] Do not add to his words, or he may rebuke you and expose you as a liar. [7] O God, I beg two favors from you; let me have them before I die. [8] First, help me never to tell a lie. Second, give me neither poverty nor riches! Give me just enough to satisfy my needs. [9] For if I grow rich, I may deny you and say, "Who is the LORD?" And if I am too poor, I may steal and thus insult God's holy name.

Yes, it's true Agur said these words and at first, they sound noble indeed! Agur is concerned that a person who has riches and wealth could deny the Lord and walk away from following Him. Although in some cases this may be true, we see many examples of Bible personalities who were rich and wealthy and still had very close relationships with the Lord.

Interestingly, Agur described himself as "brutish, without understanding, lacking wisdom, and not knowing the holy God," so it makes sense that if this type of person were to obtain great riches and wealth, he or she could deny the Lord. For a person of this character, perhaps riches and wealth would not be in their best interest.

Proverbs 1:32 (KJV) says fools should not prosper as it would bring them destruction: "For the turning away of the simple shall slay them, and the prosperity of fools shall destroy them."

4. Aren't poverty and lack the signs of true spiritual humility?

The Bible actually teaches just the opposite. Let's look at several passages of Scripture.

Proverbs 22:4 says, "True humility and fear of the LORD lead to riches, honor, and long life." Poverty and lack are not signs of true humility.

Then there's Moses. In Numbers 12:3 it says, "Now Moses was very humble—more humble than any other person on earth." If poverty is the true sign of humility, then Moses as the most humble man on earth must have also been the poorest man on earth at the time, right?

But there are no indications from the Word that Moses was poor. In fact, we saw him grow up in Pharaoh's house, a house of wealth. But then when he reached adulthood, "he refused to be called the son of Pharaoh's daughter; choosing rather to suffer affliction with the people of God, than to enjoy the pleasures of sin for a season; esteeming the reproach of Christ greater riches than the treasures in Egypt: for he had respect unto the recompense of the reward" (Hebrews 11:24-26, KJV).

189

Moses refused the world's wealth but as we shall see, God saw to it that he was prosperous anyway! If poverty was a sign of true spiritual humility, then we would have seen Moses, of all men, demonstrating and teaching this to the Israelites.

Let's look at the life of Moses, this humble servant of God.

Exodus 3:21-22

And I will cause the Egyptians to look favorably on you. They will give you gifts when you go so you will not leave empty-handed. [22] Every Israelite woman will ask for articles of silver and gold and fine clothing from her Egyptian neighbors and from the foreign women in their houses. You will dress your sons and daughters with these, stripping the Egyptians of their wealth.

Exodus 12:35, 36

And the people of Israel did as Moses had instructed; they asked the Egyptians for clothing and articles of silver and gold. [36] The LORD caused the Egyptians to look favorably on the Israelites, and they gave the Israelites whatever they asked for. So they stripped the Egyptians of their wealth!

We see no doctrine of lack in Moses' command to Israel, and we see no evidence of poverty among the Israelites!

Two other verses of Scripture remind us that being humble and living an upright life will result in blessings and good things. Psalm 84:11 says, "For the LORD God is our sun and our shield. He gives us grace and glory. The LORD will withhold no good thing from those who do what is right," and Matthew 5:5 tells us, "God blesses those who are humble, for they will inherit the whole earth."

I'm thinking that being humble and inheriting the whole earth sounds a lot like prosperity!

LET'S GET PRACTICAL

As we conclude our study, here are a few final how-to's to put this session into practice:

1) In addition to giving your tithe to your local church, how much money can you invest in those who are needy? Decide on an amount to give monthly or annually.

2) Who is on your heart? Under privileged children? The unemployed? The hungry? The sick? Poor people in your city? Orphans in third world countries? Girls being trafficked? Those without water? Single moms or kids of divorce? Others? Listen to the promptings of the Holy Spirit and make a list.

3) Decide how you will give. You can give directly to those in need, or you can join forces with agencies, churches, or ministries that are already ministering to the people you have on your heart.

WEALTH AND GENEROSITY WRAP UP

Congratulations you made it! We have covered a lot of Bible turf and now you have a working knowledge of:

- The Life of Wealth and Generosity
- The Blessing of Tithes
- The Multiplication of the Offering
- The Investment of Alms

I hope you will review and put this material into practice again and again and help others get these important success basics, so the revival of wealth and generosity that is so desperately needed among God's people thrives and flourishes!

As we finish our study together, I pray you are encouraged by this wonderful passage in Psalm 112.

Praise the LORD!
How joyful are those who fear the LORD
    and delight in obeying his commands.
Their children will be successful everywhere;
    an entire generation of godly people will be blessed.
They themselves will be wealthy,
    and their good deeds will last forever.
Light shines in the darkness for the godly.
    They are generous, compassionate, and righteous.
Good comes to those who lend money generously
    and conduct their business fairly.
Such people will not be overcome by evil.
    Those who are righteous will be long remembered.
They do not fear bad news;
    they confidently trust the LORD to care for them.
They are confident and fearless
    and can face their foes triumphantly.
They share freely and give generously to those in need.
    Their good deeds will be remembered forever.
    They will have influence and honor.
The wicked will see this and be infuriated.
    They will grind their teeth in anger;
    they will slink away, their hopes thwarted.

JOURNAL ENTRY

To get the most out of this chapter, take a few moments to journal your thoughts and/or prayers.

_____

_____

_____

_____

_____

_____

_____

_____

_____

_____

_____

_____

_____

_____

_____

_____

CONCLUSION

Well dear friends, there you have it—a basic, but meaty, study on wealth and generosity. I hope you have enjoyed and been challenged to think, pray, ponder, and ultimately get busy doing the things you've learned in this study!

When we respond to God's generosity toward us with a generous spirit towards Him and His kingdom, it's a game changer! Can you see why I was so excited to promise you that the truth of God's Word on wealth and generosity has the potential to dramatically change your life and your future?

I trust the combination of digging into the Scriptures along with the various stories has helped you see yourself living a prosperous and generous life. I have no doubt as you consistently put these principles into practice, the Lord will help you live in His economy where getting wealth and giving generously become as natural to you as breathing!

I believe the best way to summarize our time together is by praying 3 John 2 (NKJV) over you, "Beloved, I pray that you may prosper in all things and be in health, just as your soul prospers."

In Jesus' Name. Amen!
Cheering you on!

CITATIONS

Session 1

1   "H2428 - chayil - Strong's Hebrew Lexicon (KJV)." *Blue Letter Bible*. Accessed April 21, 2016. https://www.blueletterbible.org// lang/lexicon/lexicon.cfm?Strongs=H2428&t=KJV

2   "H7965 - shalowm - Strong's Hebrew Lexicon (KJV)." *Blue Letter Bible*. Accessed April 21, 2016. https://www.blueletterbible.org// lang/lexicon/lexicon.cfm?Strongs=H7965&t=KJV

3   "G2137 - euodoō - Strong's Greek Lexicon (KJV)." *Blue Letter Bible*. Accessed April 21, 2016. https://www.blueletterbible.org//lang/lexicon/ lexicon.cfm?Strongs=G2137&t=KJV

4   "H6238 - `ashar - Strong's Hebrew Lexicon (KJV)." *Blue Letter Bible*. Accessed April 21, 2016. https://www.blueletterbible.org//lang/lexicon/ lexicon.cfm?Strongs=H6238&t=KJV

5   "H3276 - ya`al - Strong's Hebrew Lexicon (KJV)." *Blue Letter Bible*. Accessed April 21, 2016. https://www.blueletterbible.org//lang/lexicon/ lexicon.cfm?Strongs=H3276&t=KJV

6   "G4053 - perissos - Strong's Greek Lexicon (KJV)." *Blue Letter Bible.* Accessed April 21, 2016. https://www.blueletterbible.org//lang/lexicon/lexicon.cfm?Strongs=G4053&t=KJV

7   "H3254 - yacaph - Strong's Hebrew Lexicon (KJV)." *Blue Letter Bible.* Accessed April 21, 2016. https://www.blueletterbible.org//lang/lexicon/lexicon.cfm?Strongs=H3254&t=KJV

8   "H7235 - rabah - Strong's Hebrew Lexicon (KJV)." *Blue Letter Bible.* Accessed April 21, 2016. https://www.blueletterbible.org//lang/lexicon/lexicon.cfm?Strongs=H7235&t=KJV

9   "G2592 - karpophoreō - Strong's Greek Lexicon (KJV)." *Blue Letter Bible.* Accessed April 21, 2016. https://www.blueletterbible.org//lang/lexicon/lexicon.cfm?Strongs=G2592&t=KJV

10   "H7399 - rĕkuwsh - Strong's Hebrew Lexicon (KJV)." *Blue Letter Bible.* Accessed April 21, 2016. https://www.blueletterbible.org//lang/lexicon/lexicon.cfm?Strongs=H7399&t=KJV

11   "H3426 - yesh - Strong's Hebrew Lexicon (KJV)." *Blue Letter Bible.* Accessed April 28, 2016. https://www.blueletterbible.org//lang/lexicon/lexicon.cfm?Strongs=H3426&t=KJV

12   "H214 - 'owtsar - Strong's Hebrew Lexicon (KJV)." Blue Letter Bible. Accessed April 21, 2016. https://www.blueletterbible.org//lang/lexicon/lexicon.cfm?Strongs=H214&t=KJV

13   "H7919 - sakal - Strong's Hebrew Lexicon (KJV)." Blue Letter Bible. Accessed April 21, 2016. https://www.blueletterbible.org//lang/lexicon/lexicon.cfm?Strongs=H7919&t=KJV

14   Dake, Finis J. *God's Plan for Man.* Lawrenceville, GA: Dake Bible Sales, 1949, 211 & 213

Session 2

1 "H214 - 'owtsar - Strong's Hebrew Lexicon (KJV)." *Blue Letter Bible.* Accessed April 21, 2016. https://www.blueletterbible.org//lang/lexicon/lexicon.cfm?Strongs=H214&t=KJV

2 Stone, Perry. "Is There a Korban in the House?" *Voice of Evangelism.* Accessed April 21, 2016. https://www.voe.org/files/3103_article.pdf

Session 4

1 "G1654 - eleēmosynē - Strong's Greek Lexicon (KJV)." *Blue Letter Bible.* Accessed April 21, 2016. https://www.blueletterbible.org//lang/lexicon/lexicon.cfm?Strongs=G1654&t=KJV

SPECIAL THANK YOUS

They say, "Teamwork makes the dream work!" and that's absolutely true about this book! While I was hunkered down on my laptop writing, these people were working wonders to help me.

Troy and Joyce Wormell, thank you for publishing the Word and leading Harrison House Publishers into a bright future.

Julie Werner, thank you for being the talented, helpful, patient managing editor that you are. Hard to believe we've worked together on books for over 15 years! You are such a joy to work with. Thank you for believing in the book and me!

Makenzie, thank you for your excellent skills in editing and making my words make sense!

Mr. John Wright, in your memory, I thank you for being the first person to teach me about living a life of wealth and generosity when you graciously supported my trip to share the gospel at Daytona Beach with Campus Crusade for Christ.

Rev. Tony Cooke, thank you for sharing your expertise and for providing your insights on Session 2, The Blessing of Tithing.

Many Delta Airlines flights, numerous Starbucks, various hotels, our sunroom and other random places where I spent hours creating, writing and editing this book, thank you for existing!

Mary Jo Fox, Kathy Marble, Tonya Nielsen, Jennifer Palthe, Marcia Hageman, and other faithful prayer partners, thank you for your consistent prayers. Thank you for taking me on as your assignment. I have no words to adequately express my deep heartfelt appreciation; I know the Lord keeps good records.

Tara Danielle, thank you for being the world's best assistant and always being one step ahead!

Carol Barker, thank you for being an amazing single mom to Rhonda, Kelly, Michelle, and I, and for instilling in us the belief that all things are possible. You taught us how to value a dollar, how to save, how to be content and make the most of what we had, how to think outside of the box, and how to have a strong work ethic. You were the best example of all of these things!

Jeff Jones, Meghan and Brodie Hock, Annie Jones, Luke and Kelsey Jones, and Eric Jones, thank you for being God's most generous gifts in my life. Love you forever.

ABOUT THE AUTHOR

Beth Jones is an author, teacher, and pastor. She and her husband, Jeff, founded and have served as the senior pastors of Valley Family Church in Kalamazoo, Michigan, since 1991. Beth also leads *The Basics with Beth,* a ministry outreach dedicated to helping people *get the basics.*

Beth grew up in Lansing, Michigan, and was raised as a Catholic. At the end of her freshman year in college, she came into a personal relationship with Christ through the testimony of her roommate. It was there, at age 19, she realized God's plan for her to preach and teach the gospel through writing and speaking. She has been following that call ever since.

Beth is the author of over 20 books including the popular *Getting a Grip on the Basics* and numerous other Basics book series, which are being used by thousands of churches in America, have been translated into over a dozen foreign languages, and are being used around the world. Beth, along with her husband and children, writes, *The Basics Daily Devo*, a free, daily email devotional for thousands of subscribers.

For over 30 years, Beth has been helping people learn the basics of their faith to build a strong foundation for their Christian lives. Beth's simple and entertaining teaching style makes learning God's Word a joy, and her passion for helping people get the basics is contagious!

She received her undergraduate degree from Boston University in Boston, Massachusetts, and received her ministry training at Rhema Bible Training Center in Tulsa, Oklahoma.

Beth and Jeff have a growing family with two daughters, two sons, one-son-in-law, one daughter-in-law, and their teacup poodle, Jonesie.

To subscribe to the free *Basics Daily Devo*
or to see more of Beth's resources, please visit:

www.bethjones.org

PRAYER OF SALVATION

God loves you—no matter who you are, no matter what your past. God loves you so much that he gave his one and only begotten Son for you. The Bible tells us that "... whoever believes in him shall not perish but have eternal life" (John 3:16 NIV). Jesus laid down His life and rose again so that we could spend eternity with Him and experience His absolute best on earth. If you would like to receive Jesus into your life, say the following prayer out loud and mean it in your heart.

Heavenly Father, I come to you admitting that I am a sinner. Right now, I choose to turn away from sin, and I ask you to cleanse me of all unrighteousness. I believe that Your son, Jesus, died on the cross to take away my sins. I also believe that he rose again from the dead so that I might be forgiven of my sins and made righteous through faith in him. I call upon the name of Jesus Christ to be the Savior and Lord of my life. Jesus, I choose to follow You and ask You that You fill me with the power of the Holy Spirit. I declare that right now I am a child of God. I am free from sin and full of the righteousness of God. I am saved in Jesus' name. Amen.

If you prayed this prayer to receive Jesus Christ as your Savior for the first time, please contact us to receive a free book by writing to us.

www.harrisonhouse.com
Harrison House
PO Box 35035
Tulsa, Oklahoma 74153

The Harrison House Vision

Proclaiming the truth and the power

Of the Gospel of Jesus Christ

With excellence;

Challenging Christians to

Live victoriously,

Grow spiritually,

Know God intimately.